WALKING ANCIENT TRACKWAYS

WALKING ANCIENT TRACKWAYS

Michael Dunn

DAVID & CHARLES
Newton Abbot   London
North Pomfret (Vt)

TO SARAH

(*title page*) Looking south along the Old Portway from Harthill Moor

Photographs by Chris and Mike Dunn
Line illustrations by David Birchall
Maps by Chris Dunn

British Library Cataloguing in Publication Data

Dunn, Michael, 1948–
  Walking ancient trackways.
  1. Trails—Great Britain—Guide-books
  2. Great Britain—Description and travel—
  1971– —Guide-books
  I. Title
  914.1 DA 600

ISBN 0-7153-8640-9

Typeset by Typesetters (Birmingham) Limited,
Smethwick, Warley, West Midlands
and printed in Great Britain
by Butler & Tanner Limited, Frome and London
for David & Charles Publishers plc
Brunel House Newton Abbot Devon

Published in the United States of America
by David & Charles Inc
North Pomfret Vermont 05053 USA

CONTENTS

Boundary stone,
Wansford Bridge.

1
ANCIENT WALKS –
AND HOW TO WALK THEM

Thousands of miles of ancient trackways, ranging from prehistoric ridgeways and Roman roads to Saxon herepaths and saltways and medieval packhorse trails, survive in the British countryside. The thirty-four walks selected for inclusion in this book include the spectacular and well known – along the superbly preserved embankment of the Roman Ackling Dyke in Dorset, for example, or across the Cheviots on Clennell Street, one of the venerable border routes connecting the Scottish borders with Northumberland – and also less famous but no less rewarding routes, such as the Kerry Hills ridgeway in the Welsh Marches or the Old Portway, used by both prehistoric and Saxon traders travelling through Derbyshire.

Many of these old routeways appear as footpaths, bridleways or country lanes on modern Ordnance Survey maps. The more well known among them – the Ridgeway, the Icknield Way and many of the Roman roads – are specifically marked, while for others more cryptic labelling points to the course of an ancient route: for example, 'Salter's Hill' and similar place-names indicate the course of a saltway. A final group of routes has to be traced more laboriously using documentary evidence and detective work; a good example is the medieval road through Cambridgeshire.

Whilst it is tempting to classify the walks on an historical basis, this would be entirely misleading. Admittedly some of the routes were primarily used in one period, but the vast majority were used by a succession of travellers over many centuries. Ackling Dyke, a superb stretch of Roman road running through Cranborne Chase in Dorset, is one example of a road which was specifically constructed for one purpose and appears to have been abandoned once its raison d'être disappeared; its magnificent agger (embankment) has probably survived only because it lay undisturbed after Cranborne Chase became a royal hunting ground.

A number of other Roman roads suffered the same fate: the road between Maidstone and Bodiam – part of a Roman route across Kent and Sussex – is barely traceable in some sections, and the Roman route from Neath to Brecon is equally difficult to follow in some parts of its journey across the Brecon Beacons. And other roads, too, belong to only one period, at least as through routes. These include the saltway southwards from Droitwich to the Thames (whose middle section, from Bourton-on-the-Hill to Westcote, is described in this book) and the Old Road, a late-eighteenth-century creation of Lord Penrhyn which opened up his estates in Snowdonia but was superseded very quickly by a turnpike road following a different route.

Nevertheless these are the exceptions rather than the rule, and an example will serve to illustrate this. Sewstern Lane in eastern Leicestershire is typical, having originated as a prehistoric track following the high ground between the Trent and Welland valleys but having also been used (at least in its southern parts) by the Romans, then by medieval traders travelling between the markets at Nottingham and Stamford, the Dukes of Rutland on their way from Belvoir Castle to London, and eighteenth-century drovers.

This succession of different uses is neither unusual nor very surprising – after all, once a track existed it made sense to use it unless conditions changed. One important change which ended the pre-eminence of pre-historic routes such as the Ridgeway and the Icknield Way was forest clearance from Roman times onwards, which allowed the previously impassable plains below the chalk ridges of southern England to be exploited. In general, however, once a line had been defined it continued to attract travellers centuries after the initial reasons for its creation had disappeared.

One result of this confusion of uses is that many ancient trackways are commonly credited to travellers who were merely re-using an existing route. The most famous example is the Pilgrims' Way through Surrey and Kent, whose name reflects its use by visitors to the shrine of St Thomas at Canterbury but which was in existence in prehistoric times as the most important route west from the Kent coast to Salisbury Plain. In Scotland, General Wade's military roads, often assumed to be eighteenth-century creations, generally re-used drovers' or whisky-smugglers' tracks through the glens and over passes such as the Corrieyairack. And in the North York Moors the Hambleton drove road, though it acquired its name and attained its greatest popularity at the height of the droving trade, was part of another very early ridgeway.

The Selected Walks

The thirty-four walks are therefore not categorised in any way, except that they are presented in roughly geographical order, beginning in south-east England and proceeding west and north to arrive finally in north-west Scotland. They vary from challenging expeditions over mountainous terrain (the High Street walk and the journey along the military road from Bridge of Orchy to Fort William spring to mind) and long, undulating walks including

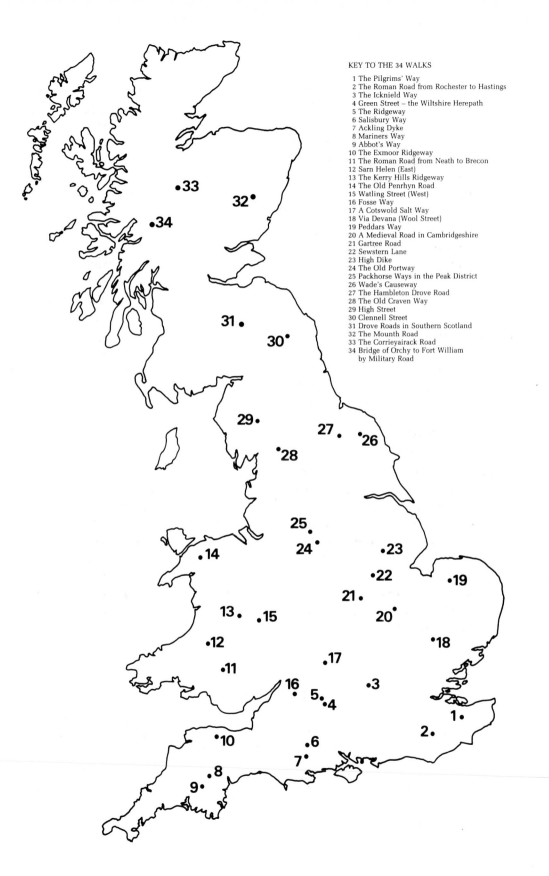

KEY TO THE 34 WALKS

1 The Pilgrims' Way
2 The Roman Road from Rochester to Hastings
3 The Icknield Way
4 Green Street – the Wiltshire Herepath
5 The Ridgeway
6 Salisbury Way
7 Ackling Dyke
8 Mariners Way
9 Abbot's Way
10 The Exmoor Ridgeway
11 The Roman Road from Neath to Brecon
12 Sarn Helen (East)
13 The Kerry Hills Ridgeway
14 The Old Penrhyn Road
15 Watling Street (West)
16 Fosse Way
17 A Cotswold Salt Way
18 Via Devana (Wool Street)
19 Peddars Way
20 A Medieval Road in Cambridgeshire
21 Gartree Road
22 Sewstern Lane
23 High Dike
24 The Old Portway
25 Packhorse Ways in the Peak District
26 Wade's Causeway
27 The Hambleton Drove Road
28 The Old Craven Way
29 High Street
30 Clennell Street
31 Drove Roads in Southern Scotland
32 The Mounth Road
33 The Corrieyairack Road
34 Bridge of Orchy to Fort William
   by Military Road

the Icknield Way and the Corrieyairack Road, to gentle strolls such as the Wiltshire Herepath and the Cotswold saltway.

In south-east and southern England the walks include a section of the Pilgrims' Way along the foot of the North Downs escarpment, the forgotten Roman road southwards from Maidstone to Bodiam, and parts of the Ridgeway and the Roman route south-west from Old Sarum along Ackling Dyke to Badbury Rings. In the south-west the choice ranges from the exposed, rough uplands traversed by the Exmoor Ridgeway to the solitude of the Abbot's Way across southern Dartmoor and the Devon lanes and paths forming part of the Mariners Way between Bideford and Dartmouth.

Wales has the extraordinary Roman road across the Brecon Beacons, the mysteries of Sarn Helen and the comparatively modern Old Road in Snowdonia; the West Midlands can lay claim to much of the Kerry Hills ridgeway (one of a number of claimants to the title of 'the oldest road'), the Roman frontier route of Watling Street (West) through the Welsh Marches, and a Cotswold saltway emanating from Droitwich. Further east are more Roman roads, a fascinating piece of detective work tracing a medieval road through the countryside near Peterborough, and an outstanding walk along Sewstern Lane, the successive uses of which are described above.

Perhaps the greatest variety of routes occurs in northern England. The range extends from Wade's Causeway, where a section of the Roman road high on the North York Moors has been laid bare and is maintained as an ancient monument, to the packhorse routes of the Dark Peak, including the magnificent track from Hayfield to Edale and Castleton – don't miss the marvellous section east of Edale Cross, where the original zigzag used by the packhorse trains above Jacob's Ladder has been laid bare by subsequent erosion. Other routes worth a special mention are Clennell Street, one of a number of fine routes across the border in the Cheviot Hills, and High Street, a remarkable Roman road rising to 2,700ft as it crosses the substantial mountain barrier of the eastern Lake District.

The Scottish countryside is threaded with ancient routeways, of which only a sample can be included: two of the eighteenth-century military roads which upgraded existing drovers' tracks through the hills, from Bridge of Orchy to Fort William and from Laggan Bridge to Fort Augustus over the daunting Corrieyairack Pass; one of the Mounth tracks, rising to 3,000ft on the Braes of Angus and used in its time by shepherds, smugglers and royalty; and one example of the many drove roads in southern Scotland, heading south from Peebles towards the border.

Practical Aspects

The logistics of walking many of the routes are comparatively simple, and most of them can comfortably be completed, and public transport reached if necessary, in the course of a single day. In these cases notes on accommodation would be superfluous. A few of the longer or more remote walks, however, are so difficult to reach by public transport, or take so long to complete, that some indication of the type and amount of available accommodation at each end of the route might be useful. Generally this is to be found at the end of the route description, and is limited to comments on the quantity of available hotels, pubs or bed-and-breakfast accommodation, although on a few occasions mention is made of particular establishments in especially remote areas.

Brief notes are provided for each walk outlining the extent of public transport provision in the vicinity of the route. The information is, of course, subject to rapid change, and never more so than at present, with the current deregulation of bus services likely to throw the whole system into confusion. The basic principle is to check before travelling – especially before relying on a service from a remote location.

Information on rail services is easily obtained, whereas details of bus services in the countryside are often appallingly difficult to track down, not least because of the plethora of very small bus companies operating in rural areas. However, county councils are obliged to co-ordinate public transport in their areas, and many have established public transport sections; almost without exception I have found their staff to be knowledgeable, friendly and helpful, and I would recommend an approach to the appropriate county council office as the best method of obtaining information.

Having arrived at the start of a walk, whether by public transport or not, the next problem is to stick to the line of the route. In some cases, especially on open moorland or where straight-as-a-die Roman roads have been fossilised in the landscape by enclosure and now appear as paths running between mature hedgerows, this is not a problem. In the intensively farmed countryside of lowland Britain matters tend to be less clear-cut, and very often the path disappears or is ploughed out, or worse still is overgrown or blatantly obstructed with barbed wire.

The two necessities in this situation are perseverance and a good map. Perseverance because on the far side of the barbed wire the path may reappear and offer a good walk – Watling Street (West) has a good example of this – and because obstructed or ploughed-out paths need to be reported and remedial work carried out before they disappear from the landscape. And a good map to ensure, amongst other things, that the right route *is* being followed: all the routes included in the book are, of course, designed to follow rights of way, which are identified on OS maps.

Each walk in this book is accompanied by a sketch map whose main purpose is to show the line of the route (a continuous line denotes a road, a broken line a path), towns or villages on or near to it, and significant landmarks mentioned in the text. The maps are based, with permission, on the Ordnance Survey maps but they are not intended to act as more than a general guide, and for detailed route-finding purposes the appropriate OS maps (which are noted at the end of each walk) should be consulted. The ideal map will in general be the relevant sheet in the 1:50,000 Landranger series, especially where the walk is long-established and popular; for some walks the 1:25,000 maps (including those of the Outdoor Leisure series which covers many tourist areas) constitute an attractive alternative, and in a few cases (noted individually) they are essential to enable the route to be followed with any confidence.

However good the chosen map is, it will be of limited value unless the symbols on it are understood and it can be used to navigate in less-than-perfect weather conditions or when the unexpected causes a change of route. Naturally, within the thirty-four walks there are wide variations: much of the Ridgeway Path, Ackling Dyke or the Corrieyairack Road can be followed without reference to maps, but on most of the routes there are crucial direction changes or unexpected choices which have to be made.

Consider carefully whether a particular walk is suitable for a particular party. Too often the chosen walk lies beyond the capabilities of the weakest member of the party, with consequent problems of fatigue and timetabling. Most of the walks in this book are comparatively 'easy' for a fit adult – indeed some, such as the Wiltshire Herepath, are no more than an afternoon stroll – but they may be much more demanding for the very young, the old or the unfit. Equally, several walks are serious expeditions not only because of their length but because of the lack of escape routes which can be used to shorten the walk: once launched on the Corrieyairack walk for example, the walker is committed to finishing it. Inevitably there is an element of risk in the longer or more exposed walks, but provided that sufficient knowledge and resources are available to deal with the unexpected, whether it is a twisted ankle, deteriorating weather or whatever, the risk can be minimised and an exhilarating, safe walk enjoyed.

2

THE PILGRIMS' WAY

Eastwell to Hollingbourne 11 miles/18km

Although the name derives from its use in the Middle Ages by pilgrims en route to the shrine of St Thomas at Canterbury the Pilgrims' Way was in use in prehistoric times as a dry route along the southern slope of the North Downs from the east Kent coast to Maidstone, Dorking and Guildford. The selected portion of the trackway provides a magnificent walk – also followed by the North Downs Way long-distance footpath – below the crest of the chalk ridge, often on tracks through beech woods or with panoramic southerly views.

Historical Background

The so-called Pilgrims' Way seems to have originated in neolithic times as a major route penetrating southern England from the obvious point of entry to the country, the Straits of Dover. Ivan Margary, in *Roman Ways in the Weald*, describes it as 'the most important prehistoric thoroughfare in the south-east of Britain'. When the Belgae established settlements in east Kent they undoubtedly used the track aligned along the North Downs scarp slope – not on the crest of the ridge, where the clay-with-flints overlying the chalk would make the going very sticky in winter, but on better-drained ground towards its base. Later, during the Roman invasion, the ancient trackway was almost certainly used by the advancing army, although once they had secured control the Romans quickly established a more direct route through Kent to London.

The westerly extension of the North Downs trackway, now called the Harrow Way, ran from Farnham to Salisbury Plain, but gradually fell into disuse from Roman times onwards and is now difficult to trace in places. East of Farnham the route remained in use, for a number of reasons: pilgrimages to the shrine of St Thomas at Canterbury (discussed below), movement between the archbishop's palaces at Charing, Maidstone and elsewhere, use by drovers and packhorse trains avoiding toll roads, and transportation of chalk or lime from the numerous chalk-pits in the North Downs along the line of the trackway.

It appears that the shrine of St Thomas à Becket became a focal point for pilgrimages very soon after his murder on 29 December 1170. Fifty years later, 7 July had become a particular date for visits to his shrine, although before long pilgrimages were spread over much of the summer season. Nevertheless it was many centuries before the name of the road was generally accepted as the Pilgrims' Way (as late as the end of the eighteenth century only one small section of the way was described as such) and although the notion spread in Victorian times it was not until Hilaire Belloc's *The Old Road* was published in 1904 that the name was popularised and romanticised.

Description of the Route

Of the various ways of reaching Eastwell church (TR009473) the most pleasant is perhaps that along the North Downs Way from Boughton Lees, passing Eastwell Park and skirting the lake. More picturesque is the walk along the lane from Eastwell Court, with the church seen superbly across Eastwell Lake on the final stage of the journey. When approaching from this direction the discovery that the church is in ruins, with only the tower standing (the remainder collapsed in 1951, after being weakened during World War II) comes as something of a shock.

The immediate area around the church is pockmarked with Eastwell Park's 'private' and 'keep out' notices, and walkers are guided none too subtly across a private drive and into a seemingly interminable field, across

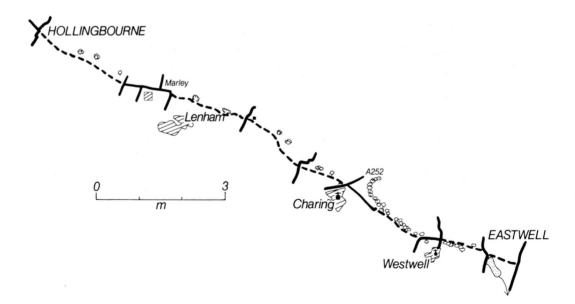

The ruined church of St Mary, Eastwell, seen across Eastwell Lake

which the way is very obvious as it approaches a strip of woodland. Climb a
stile here, walk along the south side of the wood and then pass through the
woodland to join a track running along its northern edge – a sign that modern
routes have strayed from the original line of the ancient road at this point.
Excellent views to the scarp slope of the North Downs can be rather spoilt by
the chalky whiteness of the freshly ploughed and very large fields which run
right up to the scarp at this point.

The Pilgrims' Way (and North Downs Way) uses the farm track to reach the
tiny hamlet of Dunn Street, then keeps to a narrow lane for about ½ mile,
with an improving prospect southwards across the shallow upper valley of

the Stour. In the foreground is the less imposing straggle of Westwell village, its attractive Early English church not particularly prominent. There was a mill with a fine overshot water-wheel here, but this is now a private house.

Where the road from Dunn Street swings quite sharply left the Pilgrims' Way keeps straight on, accompanied at first by a strange overgrown ravine to the left – apparently an ancient chalk working. The next mile or so is truly delightful, as the trackway twists and turns through beech woods, keeping just above the base of the scarp but with glimpses of arable fields on the left. Sadly this superb section of the walk comes to an abrupt end when the path joins the strikingly white access road of Beacon Hill Quarry and its associated limeworks. The way lies along the whitened road, past Burnt-house Farm and towards Charing Hill; on the left a footpath leads to Pett Place and Charing.

Charing, by-passed by major roads, has the outward appearance of a village but the feel of a small country town. Partly this is due to the survival of fragments of its archbishop's palace, built in the first half of the fourteenth century. The ivy-covered gatehouse, porter's lodge and a range of domestic buildings still stand, and the external walls of the palace can still be traced in places. Its Great Hall, where Henry VII dined in 1507, is now a barn. More prominent these days is the Perpendicular tower of Charing church. Behind the church is a fine medieval vicarage, and in the High Street delightful black-and-white timbering and Georgian town houses vie for attention.

Those who choose not to visit Charing will trace the Pilgrims' Way past Lonebarn to Charing Hill and the A252 crossing; less hurried pilgrims can join them here by following Charing's High Street. The sound of traffic on the main road is particularly obtrusive as it climbs the steep hill on to the downs, but thankfully it can quickly be left behind by taking the lane leading straight across the A252, past some isolated houses and above fields which, when I walked this way in April, were in use as a point-to-point steeplechase course. The lane soon degenerates into a narrow path (though with sub-stantial evidence of the passage of horses) confined by barbed wire between fields and woods rising to the crest of the North Downs.

Look back east to Charing to see the total domination of the skyline exerted by its church tower; south is the A20, the busy and excessively noisy route to the Channel ports. At Hart Hill the route negotiates a crooked crossroads and becomes much more open, with fine views ahead of the North Downs escarpment: the route of the Pilgrims' Way is clearly visible in the middle of this panorama. The way passes through a surprisingly small gate, then a welcome glade of trees, and then steers a course across prairie country, crossing a remarkably large field next to a butchered hedgerow and finally reaching Cobham Farm.

To the west of the farm the route lies along a wide dusty track across one field, then reverts to a narrow path passing close to Lenham hospital and crossing a minor road leading to Warren Street. In the vicinity of a few houses the way assumes the status of a minor road, then takes on the form of a gravel path for a while before joining a wide road close to several quite big abandoned chalk quarries. The Pilgrims' Way leaves this road to the right, along a tree-shaded lane, then becomes a footpath crossing a field in which a notice announces, in the tradition of south-east England, that 'Dogs will be shot.'

The way is now passing through sheep country, with large tracts of rough grazing, one of which contains Lenham Cross, cut immediately after World War I in memory of Lenham's war dead; a war memorial lies at the foot of the cross, together with a rather incongruous trough protected by scaffolding poles. A well-marked bridleway leads from below the cross to Lenham village, which is well worth seeing. Centred round an attractive square, Lenham is essentially a medieval market town which never really consoli-

Hedgerows mark the course of the Pilgrims' Way near Court Farm, above Harrietsham

dated its early growth. The best features are the church, the late-medieval timber-framed buildings and the weatherboarded Dog and Bear, with its excellent Shepherd Neame ales.

The Pilgrims' Way passes some unappealing modern housing west of Lenham Cross, then runs between the wholly uninviting rear façade of the Marley tile factory and the hamlet which gave the company its name. Marley Court, to the north of the lane, is an eighteenth-century farmhouse on a much older site. The lane leads past a poultry farm, then climbs gradually with a fine view of the tower of Harrietsham church on the left, to pass Stede Hill (a mansion whose parkland had inexplicably been ploughed up when I saw it).

At a crossroads south-west of Stede Hill the route runs straight on again, along a narrow metalled lane until, at the point where a tree-lined avenue comes up from Harrietsham, a track drops down quite steeply, leading well to the north of the far-from-picturesque silos and outbuildings of Court Farm. Much better are the views north-west along the chalk scarp from the trackway, which is here a white and slightly sunken lane to begin with, and then a really attractive tree-fringed lane on a shelf above yet another huge field. To the right is the big green tree-fringed bowl of a valley below Salisbury Wood; the track descends steeply to cross the valley, where there is no obvious stream, then runs along the southern side of more woodland before emerging into yet another astonishingly large ploughed field.

Hollingbourne, at the far end of the field, is reached via a lane emerging near the Pilgrim's Rest (TQ845553). The village stretches for a mile to the south, its notable buildings including an Elizabethan manor house converted into flats, a Perpendicular church and several Georgian buildings – one or two of them now functioning as pubs. The railway station, with its regular service to London, lies right in the middle of the straggling village, and is therefore ideally situated for the end of a day on the Pilgrims' Way.

Notes

Maps   OS 1:50,000 sheet 189 and a very small part of sheet 188.
Further reading   Sean Jennett, *The Pilgrims' Way* (Cassell, 1971); C. J. Wright, *A Guide to the Pilgrims' Way and North Downs Way* (Constable, 1971).
Public transport   Two buses a day run from Ashford to Eastwell and Westwell; Boughton Lees has eight buses a day on the Ashford to Faversham service. Alternatively, Wye station (2 miles from Boughton Lees) has an hourly train service from London Victoria via Ashford. Hollingbourne has hourly trains on the same service, so that a 'circular' tour is quite feasible.

3

THE ROMAN ROAD
FROM ROCHESTER TO HASTINGS

Amberfield to Bodiam 17 miles/27km

Much of the interest of this walk (partly on metalled roads and therefore easily followed by motorists too) lies in detecting the Roman route – a 'commercial' road designed to open up iron-mining areas – as it traverses the Wealden countryside of Kent and Sussex. It starts well, descending the little-known but especially attractive ragstone ridge south-east of Maidstone; it then fades into suburbia around Staplehurst, passes close to the remarkable Sissinghurst Castle and ends with the very different beauty of Bodiam Castle.

Historical Background

Before the coming of the Romans the Weald was very thinly populated, although there was a small Celtic iron industry on the northern fringes of the area, mainly supplying a local market. The Romans, too, made no real inroads into the heavily forested Silva Anderida – which the Saxons translated as Andredsweald, 'the wood where no one lives' – with the exception of a more thoroughly commercial exploitation of the iron reserves of the area. This industrial development needed roads, although not to the same high standards and rigid straightness as the military roads further north and west; the most important of them ran south from Rochester and Maidstone towards Hastings, and near Benenden was joined by a road penetrating the forest from Tenterden.

The Romans smelted the iron using charcoal as fuel, which led to considerable deforestation. Originally they worked on remarkably pure iron ore (up to 55 per cent iron content), smelting it in bloomeries and producing large quantities of waste products, mainly iron slag, which was so hard that they used it as a base for their local roads. Much of the iron was exported from Bodiam (then on the Rother estuary) and transported long distances by the Roman fleet – a hoard of a million Wealden nails has been found at Inchtuthil in Scotland. The Roman iron industry appears to have lasted for about two hundred years, and then to have died out quite suddenly, possibly because the reserves of rich and easily accessible ore had been exhausted.

19

The end of Roman interest in the Weald was followed by a long period of peace in the forest. Slowly, however, Saxon settlers established themselves there, feeding their hogs on the acorns and at first allowing them to roam freely. Later, separate enclosures or 'dens' were created and from these hog-breeding pastures evolved the forest settlements such as Elderden, Comenden, Chittenden and Benenden – all on the line of the Roman road.

The Kentish Weald was still a sparsely populated backwater, however, and it remained that way until the fourteenth century, when the cloth trade was introduced and Flemish weavers were imported into the area around Cranbrook. Later still, the iron industry was revived, this time using water-power for its furnaces and forges, but still requiring the destruction of the remaining forest cover as fuel for its fires. The Wealden landscape became one of small fields and copses rather than extensive woodland – but by now parts of the Roman road were no more than a relict feature in the landscape, for its use as a through route had long since been abandoned.

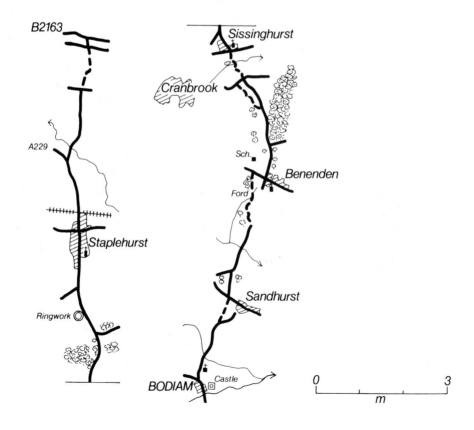

Description of the Route

Parts of the Roman road south from Rochester and through Maidstone are very clear – near Blue Bell Hill and around Mangravet cemetery, for example – but other sections are very difficult to trace, and for this reason the recommended walk begins near Amberfield (TQ799503), south of the B2163. The first mile or so is delightful, and is an illustration of the fact that this is a Roman road which adapts to the terrain rather than adopting a rigidly straight course. For a short distance the Roman road is represented by a bridleway running south across the plateau through apple orchards, but at a crossroads of tracks the Romans had to negotiate the steep descent from the ragstone ridge into the valley of the Beult. They achieved this by means of a curving holloway; its depth is made even more impressive nowadays by later agricultural use but it is nevertheless a fine example of Roman ingenuity.

The way emerges at the bottom of the escarpment as a caked mud track passing between an orchard and a cornfield (there is a fine retrospective view of the ragstone ridge, with a curving hedgerow marking the course of the Roman road, from the far end of the field) and then approaches Hermitage Corner as a green lane beneath an avenue of trees. To the east of the road junction there is a half-timbered cottage, to the west an intensive poultry unit. Straight ahead lies the narrow road marking the Roman route; at first this is a quiet country lane, but it soon joins a much busier route through Rabbits Cross and then, veering away from the Roman alignment, crosses an elaborate bridge over the River Beult to join the main road (A229) at Cross-at-Hands.

There is no great enjoyment in tramping along the A229 through Staplehurst and there will be a temptation to take the bus (reasonably frequent) towards Cranbrook. There are, however, a number of points of interest along the way. First, though, Staplehurst and its spreading suburbia, totally out of character with the older part of the village, has to be negotiated. The church is the only notable building, and that only for the elaborate twelfth-century ironwork around the doorway, decorated with iron fishes, snakes, serpents and the like.

Near the church the main road breasts a slight rise and a fine southerly prospect comes into sight, with the course of the road plainly visible for some miles across a minor valley and up through well-wooded countryside into the Weald. At Knox Bridge a ringwork, a puzzling moated feature, perhaps appears on the map more prominently than it does on the ground. As the lower slopes of the Weald are reached the Roman road climbs gradually on short alignments, altering its course frequently near Comenden Manor and Cranbrook Common to avoid crossing tributaries of the Hammer

The Roman road at Hermitage Corner, below the ragstone ridge

Stream, and then making for Sissinghurst on a line now represented by the link road east of Wilsley Pound.

Sissinghurst village is prim and proper, conscious of its proximity to the now famous castle. Yet both castle and village were until quite recently much less exalted. The village was known until the early nineteenth century as Milkhouse Street, and until 1930 the castle, to the east of the village, was little more than a ruin. Sissinghurst Castle was built in Henry VIII's reign and visited by Queen Elizabeth in 1573, but by the nineteenth century it was in use as a poorhouse. It was rescued by Vita Sackville-West and her husband, Sir Harold Nicolson, who transformed the remains of the Tudor mansion into an unusual but enchanting country house, and created the exquisite gardens around the house and its moat.

A minor road runs south from Sissinghurst to the hamlet of Golford, and the Roman road also passed through the hamlet, but it reached it by a different route. Take the unsurfaced lane heading south between cottages some thirty yards east of the Maidstone turning; fork right after a hundred yards, then keep to the left-hand edge of a very large field, heading towards a substantial tract of woodland. Go straight ahead into the woods, where the path is very obvious on the ground, winding among the trees and crossing

22

three small footbridges and some adjacent marshy areas. To the right of the path is a steep bank, and from the top of this there is the startling sight of a hidden lake embedded in the woods. Leave the woodland by surmounting a stile, then keep to a narrow path along the edge of a field, and finally swing left to meet the road as it climbs up to Golford crossroads.

A hundred yards up the road, on the right, is a cart-track, later a mere path, which roughly keeps to the Roman alignment as far as Farningham Farm. (Before taking to the track it is worth considering a detour to Coursehorn, a very fine weaver's house with its magnificent old cloth hall, a relic of the Flemish weavers, and Cranbrook, notable for its superb Perpendicular church, Union Windmill – at 70ft the highest in the Weald – and public school.) South of Farningham the line is lost and the road is the only alternative as far as Benenden, although the course of the Roman road has been located west of Chittenden and then runs through the grounds of Benenden School (formerly known as Hemsted Park).

Benenden, another well-to-do Wealden village with a history traceable through Domesday to its origins as a Saxon 'den' or swine pasture, is worth a look. Its massive triangular green, doubling as the village cricket ground, is an imposing centrepiece, but there is also the village church, which was struck by lightning in 1673, ruinous in early Victorian times and over-exuberantly restored in 1862 by the Earl of Cranbrook, together with a number of fine timber-framed and weatherboarded houses and the comfortable King William IV inn.

Go west at the Benenden crossroads until, nearly opposite the school drive, there is a path signposted on the left. This develops into an excellent green lane and later becomes a sunken holloway, often overgrown and in some places a 15ft deep ravine, descending a slope to Stream Farm, where the right of way comes to a sudden end. There was a paved Roman ford here, fashioned from sandstone blocks, but now only a few scanty remains can be seen by peering over the barbed wire. The agger can be seen beyond the stream, heading uphill to Iden Green – which is also accessible via a lesser holloway east of the farm – and then the minor road, which takes over the Roman alignment across the Hexden Channel and past Challenden to Sandhurst.

Sandhurst church, with its bulky tower, is a further mile to the south, and a fine footpath passing through orchards denotes the Roman route towards it. This was the original site of the village, but after the Black Death the survivors moved to a fresh site a safe distance away. From Sandhurst Cross the present road to Bodiam marks the course, although near the Kent Ditch crossing (the county boundary between Kent and Sussex) slag metalling has been uncovered further to the east. The footpath past Court Lodge to Bodiam

Bodiam Castle

Castle (TQ786256) now marks the road, which reached a Roman harbour here when the Rother basin was an estuary.

Bodiam is almost a toy castle, in a magnificent setting enhanced by its encircling moat and attendant trees. It was not built until the fourteenth century, ostensibly to guard the Rother crossing, but it never came under siege and retains its classic medieval battlemented symmetry and majestic corner towers. The castle suffered from neglect in the eighteenth century but is now National Trust property and is expertly manicured for the hordes of visitors which descend on it daily – a far cry from the Roman road whose neglected course we have been following.

Notes

Map OS 1:50,000 sheet 188.
Further reading Sheila Kaye-Smith, *Weald of Kent and Sussex* (Robert Hale, 1973); Ivan Margary, *Roman Roads in Britain* (John Baker, 3rd edn. 1973).
Public transport There is a two-hourly bus service from Maidstone to Chart Corner which runs along the B2163 close to the start of the walk. Bodiam has infrequent buses to Hastings (only one afternoon service). In addition, for those contemplating walking only part of the route, the Tunbridge Wells to Tenterden service calls at Benenden.

4

THE ICKNIELD WAY

Princes Risborough to Goring 20 miles/32km

The Icknield Way is, together with the Ridgeway, the best-known of Britain's prehistoric trackways. Beginning on the north Norfolk coast it runs south-west to Newmarket, Dunstable and Goring, where after crossing the River Thames it continues to Salisbury Plain and, finally, the coast near Axmouth, by which time it has joined the Ridgeway. Large parts of Icknield Way were used by the Romans, and a good deal is still in use as main roads, but the chosen stretch across the Chiltern Hills is mostly on footpaths and quiet green lanes.

Historical Background

Part of what is often referred to as the 'Oldest Road', the Icknield Way was first trodden by neolithic settlers and has since assisted a wide variety of travellers. The original direction of travel was north to south, as prehistoric man, having landed on the north coast of Norfolk, spread south and west along the base of the ridge to Newmarket and Goring. Here the barrier of the Thames had to be overcome, and the route then followed the Ridgeway to Salisbury Plain, the Dorset hills and the Axe estuary near Seaton.

At first the route lay at the base of the scarp, and it may not have served as a long-distance path at all, but merely as a track connecting adjacent farms. Gradually, however, a permanent through route was formed, and perhaps at the same time two or more parallel ways were defined. The Lower Icknield Way followed the junction of the chalk hills and the clay vale, but whilst it was closest to water sources and settlements it may have become impassable in winter. The Upper Icknield Way then came into its own, though even this higher route kept well below the top of the escarpment.

The Romans utilised parts of the existing Lower Icknield Way, straighten-ing it where necessary, and even more drastic adjustment followed at the hands of the eighteenth- and nineteenth-century surveyors during the enclosure movement. As a result much of the lower way has been altered beyond recognition and is now used by busy roads – indeed, between Baldock and Newmarket the A11 follows much of the line. But the Upper Icknield Way through the Chilterns remains as a green lane for much of its

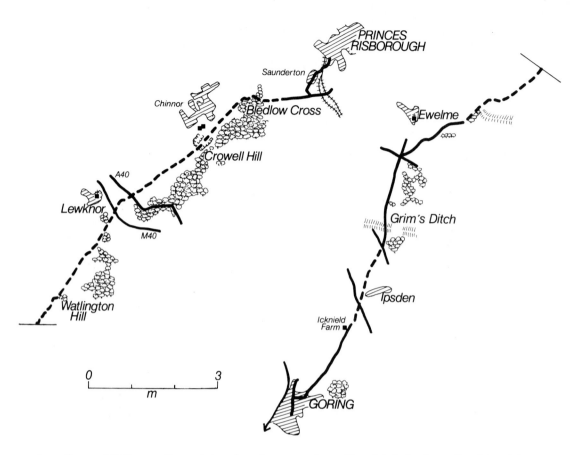

length, and it forms the setting for the superb walk which is described in this chapter.

Description of the Route

The first priority on arriving at Princes Risborough station (SP799027) will be to get out of the London suburban sprawl surrounding it. The quickest route takes the lane east of the station, signposted to Saunderton, crosses the railway, passes Saunderton church (well hidden by trees) and reaches the Upper Icknield Way, used here as a street name, north of Home Farm. At first this is a fairly busy road, but at a T-junction after ½ mile the Icknield Way continues straight ahead as a bright white cart-track, climbing steadily between tall hedges. Where a footpath goes over a stile to the right there are wide views back east along the Chiltern scarp towards Whiteleaf Cross and Pulpit Hill.

Very soon there is a choice of four paths: those to the left climb the higher reaches of Wain Hill, while the right-hand alternative drops down towards Bledlow. The sensible choice lies straight on, contouring the hill and thus conserving energy which will be needed later. The track runs between a deep combe to the right and a recent plantation high on the left, then slowly loses height and cuts through between cottages in the hamlet of Hempton Wainhill. The next ½ mile is a pleasant narrow lane through beech woods, with Bledlow Cross (of uncertain antiquity, maybe only seventeenth century) seen only with difficulty through the trees on the higher slopes.

The path widens into a broad, unsurfaced access lane for a handful of houses, and it becomes considerably harder on the feet for a while. To the right is Chinnor, site of an Iron Age settlement and with a fine church rebuilt in the 1320s, but otherwise modern, industrial and unappealing. Slightly further away are the unlovely chimney stacks of Chinnor cement works. Beyond a busy minor road the way becomes, much to the relief of the feet, a wide grassy ride between impenetrable hedges. At first this is exhilaratingly fast, comfortable walking but the lack of interest takes its toll after a while—until at a gap on the left the reason for the barrier becomes clear. The grassy ride is all that remains of the land surface here, because Chinnor Quarry extends on both sides of Icknield Way.

At last the quarry workings come to an end, and the Oxfordshire plain comes into view beyond the spring-line villages at the foot of the chalk escarpment. This is a memorable part of the walk, below the wooded Crowell Hill, with the path becoming a wide grassy lane as far as the Stokenchurch road. Beyond the road crossing, the now somewhat narrower trackway is hemmed in by the course of a dismantled railway to the right,

Icknield Way and the view north-east to Crowell Hill

beyond a thick hedge, but there is an uninterrupted view left across arable fields to the Chiltern woods on Aston Hill.

The dappled shade of a copse near Warren Farm was welcome when I walked this way on a blazing hot August day, and it also served to reduce the roar of motorway traffic. Beyond the A40, however, the sight and sound of the M40 is unavoidable. The Icknield Way approaches the motorway around the lower edge of the Beacon Hill nature reserve, 300 acres of species-rich chalk grassland with a nature trail, then passes under the M40 in an oppressively long concrete underpass. Two hundred yards further on the route crosses the Hill Farm lane, which can be followed north-west into the village of Lewknor. I found the twelfth-century church and thatched village school of considerable interest, but on such a hot day the Old Leathern Bottel and its thirst-quenching Henley Brewery bitter took precedence.

Back at the Hill Farm crossroads, turn south on to the Icknield Way, here fringed by trees for some distance. A 'no parking' sign emphasises the metropolitan character of the countryside near the M40, but after a while the way reverts to a pleasant narrow path through trees. On the right is Shirburn, most notable for its very private medieval (though much altered) castle. Pyrton, a much friendlier village, is slightly further away from the ancient route.

The Icknield Way now takes the form of a gravelly cart-track, with meadowland to the left below the wooded Chiltern scarp and cornfields dominating a wide vista over the plain. Later a green lane forms the route, curving uphill before losing height to cross the Watlington road. Those who

The Olde Leathern Bottel, Lewknor

resisted the diversion to Lewknor might find Watlington, ½ mile from the route, with its brick town hall and thatched cottages, irresistible, but the return journey is all uphill. I carried straight on to 'Icknield' on the B480, then climbed the wide metalled road to the opulent Lys Farm. The road ends here and the way undergoes yet another transformation, to a narrow and somewhat overgrown path, then widens to cross a minor road (the junction seemingly beset with parking problems) and continues to the west of North Farm.

The Ridgeway long-distance path turns left here, but the line of Icknield Way is perpetuated by the rough track which carries on past Britwell House, built by Sir Edward Simeon in the eighteenth century. The park around the house is well provided with monuments, which can easily be seen from the track. Less welcome is the first glimpse of the cooling towers of Didcot power station, constant if distant companions from now on. The track now runs by the side of a wood to reach a minor road at Sliding Hill.

For a while now the Icknield Way is represented by country lanes, the first of them running south-west from the junction on Sliding Hill to the crossroads near Blenheim Farm, and passing on the way fields full of hideous white plastic pig sties (the corrugated iron version is also quite common). The road passes a turning to Ewelme, well worth a detour if time and energy permit: the superb church with the tomb of Dame Alice de la Pole, Duchess of Suffolk, the attractive manor house, the nucleus of medieval and later cottages, and the watercress beds fed by a sparkling stream, add up to a village full of interest. Less attractive, temporarily, is the route of the Icknield Way above the village as it passes Ewelme Quarry and a generally despoiled landscape.

Matters improve quickly once the A423 and Blenheim Farm have been left behind. First, the lane passes through a gap in Grim's Ditch. Not perhaps in the Offa's Dyke class of linear earthworks, the ditch is nevertheless a compelling reminder of past endeavour, despite the fact that no one seems sure what its purpose was. As a defensive barrier it appears to have been useless, facing the wrong direction and easily being circumvented, so the theory that it was a boundary between Saxon kingdoms seems more plausible.

The second improvement is the end of the road walking at Wicks Hill. The way becomes a farm track for a matter of yards, then a narrow footpath which soon finds itself traversing an unploughed strip between massive fields, seemingly stretching to the Chiltern woods on one hand and the Berkshire Downs on the other. The Icknield Way continues ahead across a minor road, with views of Ipsden, and in particular the largest barn in England, on the left. At another road keep straight on again (even though, at least on my sun-

Grim's Ditch

drenched walk in August, the path had been ploughed out) to a gap in the far hedge; cross the A4074 and repeat the process across another ploughed field.

From now on there is nothing but road walking, past Icknield Farm and fields of remarkable size. Even the gentle gradient of Catsbrain Hill is trying at this stage of the walk, but now Goring is close at hand, beyond Grove Farm and the council estate at Cleeve. Cross the railway line (SU603808) and walk down the main street to the River Thames, with its willows, locks and weirs, then back to the church with its Norman tower, and then possibly to one of the pubs, of which the John Barleycorn is the most authentic.

Notes

Maps   OS 1:50,000 sheets 165 and 175.
Further reading   G. R. Crosher, *Along the Chiltern Ways* (Cassell, 1973); Elizabeth Cull, *Portrait of the Chilterns* (Robert Hale, 1982).
Public transport   Princes Risborough has a two-hourly Saturday and Sunday service (slightly more trains during the week) from Marylebone. Goring is served by hourly trains on the line from Paddington to Oxford. There is an express bus service from Reading to Princes Risborough which can be used to organise a 'round trip' based on Reading.

5

GREEN STREET –
THE WILTSHIRE HEREPATH

Marlborough to Avebury 7 miles/11km

This short and easy walk follows the course of the best-known herepath (Saxon military way) across the Marlborough Downs. Since it leads directly to the stone circle at Avebury it can probably claim prehistoric origins, and it was again re-used in medieval times and as late as the eighteenth century as part of the Great West Road from London to Bath.

Historical Background

Very little is known about the road system of the Dark Ages, especially about the long-distance roads which must have existed. Many Saxon charters do, however, refer to the existence of a 'Here-paeth', which is generally taken to mean a military road. Certainly many herepaths lead to the known sites of battles, but others have less obvious military uses and may well have been used for through journeys by the civilian population.

The most celebrated of the herepaths runs for 7 miles between Marlborough and Avebury; it was certainly known as such in Saxon times and was presumably then used by opposing armies after the Roman road (traces of which can still be seen on Overton Hill) fell into disuse. Like a number of other such routes, it is accorded the description 'herepath' on the Ordnance Survey map.

It is all too easy, however, to assume that the survival of Saxon references to its purpose, together with modern acceptance of its status, constitutes conclusive proof of its Dark Age origins. The path leads directly across the Marlborough Downs, pockmarked with evidence of prehistoric activity, to the stone circle at Avebury, and it is virtually certain that the trackway was in use in prehistoric times. Timperley and Brill, in fact, describe it merely as one of the Wiltshire branches of the Ridgeway, and make no reference to its later history.

Not only does the trackway predate the Saxon era by many centuries, but it was also re-used in later medieval times as one route for the Great West Road between London and Bath, and this use continued until the Kennet valley

31

alternative between Marlborough and Beckhampton, south-west of Avebury, was turnpiked in the eighteenth century. Surprisingly little evidence of this use has survived, although on Manton Down a field is still called London Road Ground. The disused road presumably earned its later name of Green Street as it became the open track across the downs which it remains today. So the 'Wiltshire Herepath', apparently a simple example of a Dark Age trackway, has as complex a history as many of the roads in this book, and it illustrates perfectly the difficulties inherent in any attempt at historical classification of ancient routeways.

Description of the Route

Faced with only a 7 miles stroll across fairly level ground, a determined walker might treat this walk as merely an aperitif for the Ridgeway walk – and indeed I have set out from a mist-shrouded Marlborough at 7.30 on a summer morning and, with only rabbits and the occasional horseman for company, approached Avebury well before 10am. But the Herepath deserves much more than that, with a wealth of interest in both Marlborough and Avebury, and racehorse gallops, Celtic fields, sarsens and burial chambers on the route itself.

Start at the west end of Marlborough High Street (SU186687), at the church of St Peter and St Paul, with its ashlar-faced Perpendicular tower and attractive tree-fringed churchyard. To the west is Marlborough College on the site of the castle. To the east is the long, wide and potentially immensely attractive High Street, mainly Georgian in character but with a few restrained modern buildings as well. The pity is that cars are allowed to park along the whole of the central island, all but destroying the sense of spaciousness and introducing danger and visual and noise pollution into the scene. Now the reasoning behind my departure so early in the morning becomes more apparent!

Walk east along the High Street, noting the Merlin Tea Rooms (Merlin is reputedly buried in the castle mound), the Georgian Restaurant and the late Georgian Ailesbury Arms Hotel on the way to the brick and stone town hall,

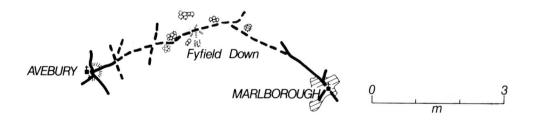

The Herepath on Manton Down, with racehorse gallops on the left

turn-of-the-century and looking a little out of place in this largely Georgian town. Fires in 1653 and later in the seventeenth century destroyed much of the old town and, incidentally, led to an Act of Parliament banning the use of thatch in Marlborough. Behind and above the town hall is Marlborough's second church, St Mary's, from whose elevated churchyard there is a fine view back along the High Street.

Go north from the town hall, following the Swindon road (A345) for ½ mile, then the Rockley road across Marlborough Common and its golf course. Where the road bends right, bear left through a gate and cross Barton Down in the company of racehorse gallops. To the right are wide vistas across cornfields to the tree-topped hills on Ogbourne Down. On the left, across the gallops, is a Roman villa site where hoards of coin and pewter have been discovered.

The track keeps straight on, with woods across the gallops to the left and a few solitary trees preserved, to the enormous benefit of the landscape, in the huge ploughed field on the right. Go straight across at a junction with a bridleway, and in a few yards, at the crest of a minor hill, the outlook improves significantly. The herepath can be seen dropping down to a wooded dell and then swinging left up to the horizon, accompanied by further gallops, which stand out as an oasis of green in the surrounding cornfields.

The gallops, highly valued because of the properties of the downland turf, are part of the Manton House complex. Formerly a top racehorse stable – the legendary George Todd once trained here – Manton House was allowed to decline, but the estate has been purchased by Robert Sangster, the millionaire pools magnate and racehorse breeder, who has established his private trainer here.

At the wooded dell a short-cut to Hackpen Hill and the Ridgeway bears off to the right; Green Street continues close to the gallops, rising over Clatford Down (the Devil's Den, a cromlech used by Thomas Hardy, who called it the Devil's Door, in 'What the Shepherd Saw', is a mile or so to the left) and into a different landscape. Gone are the ploughed fields and waving corn, replaced by rough pasture strewn with sarsen stones.

The sarsens, lichen-covered blocks of sandstone, are also called 'grey wethers' because of their similarity to reclining sheep, and indeed on a dull or misty day it can be difficult to distinguish them. The sarsens, many of which were transported in prehistoric times to Avebury or Stonehenge, were later shaped and used locally as building stone, but now form one feature of the 610 acre Fyfield Down national nature reserve. Interspersed among them are the remains of roughly rectangular Celtic field enclosures, some of them with the marks of medieval ploughing superimposed.

Green Street approaches the Ridgeway on Overton Down as an open path crossing a field littered with sarsens, but leaves it to the west as a broad and deeply rutted track enclosed between barbed wire fences. It loses height gradually at first, then more steeply (there is a fine view north of the scarp face of the Marlborough Downs and Hackpen Hill) to a junction of tracks half a mile from Avebury. Now the herepath becomes a metalled lane, passes a farm on the left and squeezes through a gap in the massive bank and ditch of Avebury stone circle. The visual shock accompanying the sudden transition from quiet rolling downland to prehistoric monument is extraordinary.

Strictly speaking the way lies straight on along the lane, past thatched cottages into the centre of the village (SU102699) but a diversion around the earthworks is more or less mandatory. Larger than Stonehenge, with an outer circle originally consisting of about a hundred undressed sarsen stones and two inner circles, the stone circle covers 29 acres and is enclosed by a bank which is still 15ft high. The site is split into four by modern roads (at least three of which are prehistoric in origin) and part of the modern village lies inside the circle.

To the south-east a stone avenue – about a hundred pairs of standing stones – leads to the Sanctuary, a ceremonial site on Overton Hill. West from here are the West Kennett long barrow, 350ft long and with five burial chambers, and Silbury Hill, man-made and obviously prehistoric since the

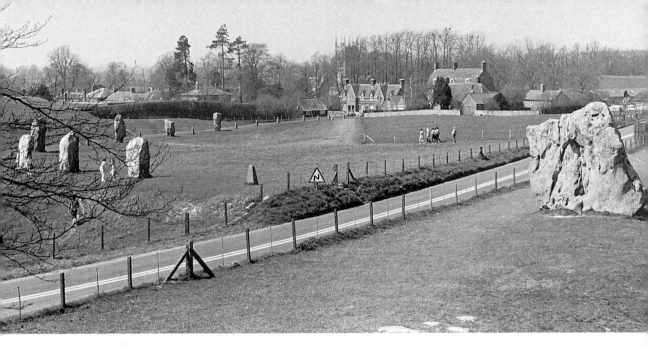

Part of the stone circle at Avebury

Roman road alters course to avoid it, but of unknown date and purpose. Finally, to the north-west of Avebury is the early-neolithic causewayed camp on Windmill Hill.

After all this the present village of Avebury is inevitably an anticlimax, although the group of parish church and Elizabethan manor house, built on the site of a Benedictine cell, is pleasant enough. To the east of the church is the Great Barn, seventeenth century and thatched, and now the home of the Wiltshire Museum of Folk Life. To the west a path leads across an ancient and narrow bridge to Trusloe Manor and the rest of the village.

Notes

Map   OS 1:50,000 sheet 173.
Further reading   Christopher Taylor, *Roads and Tracks of Britain* (Dent, 1979); H. W. Timperley and Edith Brill, *Ancient Trackways of Wessex* (Shipston-on-Stour: Drinkwater, 2nd edn. 1983).
Public transport   Both Marlborough and Avebury can be reached from Swindon. Marlborough has an hourly service on weekdays, Avebury an infrequent service.

6

THE RIDGEWAY

Overton Hill to Chiseldon 9 miles/14km

Part of the great prehistoric network of trackways which spread out from a focal point on Salisbury Plain, the Ridgeway continues the line of the Icknield Way from the Goring Gap over the Berkshire and Wiltshire Downs and across the Vale of Pewsey to the Plain. Much of it now forms part of a recognised long-distance footpath – a reflection of its outstanding recreational importance – and the selected walk follows the first few miles from Overton Hill to Barbury Castle and Chiseldon.

Historical Background

With the Icknield Way, the Ridgeway lays claim to the title of the 'Oldest Road'. In a sense this is speculation, since by definition there are no records of the prehistoric period, but it is clear that the high, dry chalk ridge from the Wash down to the Chilterns and the downlands of Berkshire and Wiltshire formed a natural high-level route for the earliest settlers. It is clear, too, that trackways such as these were in early and regular use as routes to and from the extraordinary religious centres at Stonehenge and Avebury.

Later the Ridgeway became a trade route, with stone axes and arrowheads from Wales and the Lake District conveyed here in neolithic times, and gold ornaments and copper and bronze implements in the Bronze Age. Later still, Celtic incursions in the Iron Age led to the construction of many hill-forts to defend land along the course of the Ridgeway: the fort at Barbury Castle is an excellent example, commanding the scarp and also the Ridgeway itself, which here runs immediately below the fort.

The Romans found the general direction of the Ridgeway unhelpful to their advance across southern Britain, and appear to have used little of the ancient road west of the Thames. This was the start of the route's decline into obscurity, and in more settled times farms and villages were established below the ridge, and the roads which grew up to connect them eventually superseded the Ridgeway, which was higher and more inconvenient. Even the drovers, though they made some use of the Ridgeway to avoid turnpike tolls, have not left their imprint as clearly as in, say, the Scottish glens or the Welsh Marches. Indeed, it has taken the growth of walking for pleasure to

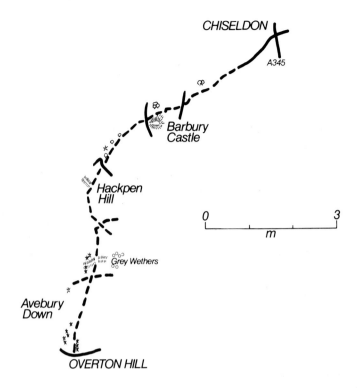

CHISELDON

A345

Barbury
Castle

Hackpen
Hill

0   3

m

Grey Wethers

Avebury
Down

OVERTON HILL

revive the old road as a through route rather than a series of farm tracks and derelict by-ways.

Description of the Route

The walk to be described extends for only 9 miles, and is designed essentially to give a taste of the pleasures of Ridgeway walking and, perhaps, to stimulate the more active walker to spend a few days walking at least as far as Goring. It starts at Overton Hill (SU119681), the location of which is unmistakable when approached from the east, with a line of round barrows extremely prominent on the crest of a spur just west of West Overton village.

This hillside and its immediate surroundings are a remarkable focus of interest for the devotee of prehistoric monuments. Just to the south is the site of the Sanctuary, a former stone circle ploughed out in the seventeenth century. Further south, below a canopy of trees, is the unexcavated East Kennett long barrow, on private land, and round to the west is the West Kennett long barrow (open to the public), with tremendous standing stones guarding the entrance to its five chambers. Next is Silbury Hill, the largest earthwork in Europe but of mysterious origin and purpose. North again, the West Kennett avenue, parallel lines of standing stones, leads to Avebury, whose stone circle has already appeared in this book, as the destination of the Green Street (Wiltshire Herepath) walk.

The Ridgeway itself runs due north at first from Overton Hill, with yet more antiquities immediately to hand. On the right are the six tumuli, in two groups of three, and in the gap between the two groups lies the course of the Roman road from London to Bath – its agger discernible in a field to the east of the Ridgeway. Behind the rather incongruous Ridgeway Café stood yet another stone circle, but all traces of this one have vanished.

There is no danger of losing the Ridgeway as it climbs gently across the southern outliers of Hackpen Hill (its flat top still some 3 miles distant), since it exists as a very broad and very rutted track, worn down to its gleaming white chalky subsoil. Beyond the sixth and final barrow there is a curious sense of anticlimax as the track negotiates a rather featureless plateau; the appearance of a clump of bushes and stunted trees ½ mile further on comes as something of a relief. To the right now are fields of weathered grey sarsen stones, part of the Fyfield Down national nature reserve.

On Avebury Down the Ridgeway intersects with Green Street, the Wiltshire Herepath, at a junction festooned with signposts and a useful nature reserve noticeboard. Still the deep ruts persist on the ancient road, a reminder that this is a by-way open to *all* traffic, including cyclists, horseriders, motorcyclists and heavy farm vehicles (and I saw all of those, together with cars in seemingly impossible places, on one journey along this short section of the Ridgeway). The path continues to climb gently to Monkton Down, then turns abruptly right and, after 200 yards, left to continue its almost imperceptible rise to the top of Hackpen Hill. On the left a solitary tumulus stands out strikingly across a ploughed field, to the left of Berwick Bassett Clump.

The landscape value of the little spinneys such as Berwick Bassett Clump is incalculable in this section around Hackpen Hill; without them the plateau would be almost featureless and the journey, on a wide green lane set well back from the scarp edge and therefore devoid of distant views, a little monotonous – though there is one enormous round barrow close at hand on the way to the top. As it is, there is another fine group of trees to aim for, at the Broad Hinton road crossing, where the track widens into an impromptu car park. Below the path, and within the hairpin bend described by the surfaced road, is a white horse, though this one dates from as recently as 1838.

There are earthworks, defined in detail on the OS map, in the arable fields to the left here, but they are disappointingly inconspicuous on the ground and in any case are difficult of access from the path, which still consists of a wide green lane, partly rutted, between wire fences. The ridge loses height slightly – a path drops down to Broad Hinton at the col – then climbs again to the northern summit of Hackpen Hill (at 883ft only 9ft lower than the highest point on this long plateau) before starting to descend Uffcott Down to the gap where the minor road from Wroughton to Marlborough climbs the scarp slope.

At the beginning of the descent there is a sudden and memorable view of Barbury Castle, its double banks and ditches seen in profile along the escarpment. Tools dating from the third century BC have been discovered at the fort, which is unexcavated, but it may also have been fleetingly re-used in AD 556, when the West Saxons gained a decisive victory over the Britons in the Battle of Beranburh, which took place on the hill slopes north of the fort. Earthworks south of Barbury Castle appear to be associated with the site of a deserted medieval village.

From the road crossing it is worth exploring the castle (which now forms part of a country park), but the path cutting through the middle of the fort, and scarring the landscape badly in the process, is not the Ridgeway (though, confusingly, it *is* the Ridgeway long-distance path, which for its own reasons parts company with the historic route for several miles). The true route of the Ridgeway lies further north, below the hill-fort, losing height gradually as it crosses Burderop Down and heads north-east to Chiseldon. Before dropping down too far, however, pause to savour for the last time the wide views north-east across the clay plain.

The Ridgeway on Hackpen Hill

Barbury Castle from the south-west

The track intersects with a country lane which was formerly the medieval coach road from Swindon to Marlborough, then follows a straight and fairly level course between Burderop Hackpen and Draycot Foliat to emerge on to a country road at a junction north of the Army's Chiseldon Camp. The first road on the left leads down into Chiseldon village (SU185795), with its thatched cottages around the church. The second road met by the lane now carrying the Ridgeway is the A345, with buses to Swindon, and the third leads to Badbury, with locally brewed Arkell's beer in the Baker's Arms. Alternatively the Ridgeway itself beckons, with Wayland's Smithy long barrow, the Uffington white horse, Segsbury Camp, the Thames at Goring . . .

Notes

Map   OS 1:50,000 sheet 173.
Further reading   Sean Jennett, *The Ridgeway Path* (HMSO, 1976); Oxfordshire County Council, *Ridgeway Information Pack* (County Council, 1984); H. W. Timperley and Edith Brill, *Ancient Trackways of Wessex* (Shipston-on-Stour: Drinkwater, 2nd edn. 1983).
Public transport   There are two buses a day (more on Wednesdays) from Marlborough via Overton Hill to Avebury. Chiseldon is served by the hourly Swindon to Marlborough bus service.

7

THE SALISBURY WAY

Whitesheet Hill to Salisbury 14 miles/22km

An exhilarating walk following the prehistoric ridgeway along the crest of the chalk ridge between the Nadder and Ebble valleys. Later the track formed part of the coach route between Exeter and London, and because of its almost continuous use it is particularly well preserved as a straight green lane.

Historical Background

Ridge-top routes of great antiquity are the rule on the Wiltshire downs, and the chalk ridges south-west of Salisbury are no exception. To the south of the Ebble valley runs the Ox Drove, a prehistoric ridgeway whose name betrays its later use. To the north the ridge route now known as the Salisbury Way had a longer history as an important road, but is now an equally quiet green lane.

The line of the Salisbury Way must have been particularly attractive to prehistoric travellers. The broad chalk ridge between two damp and forested valleys offered an open, dry passage leaving the Ridgeway itself near Win Green and heading for the Avon valley and the routes to the east. The siting of the Iron Age village on Swallowcliffe Down, just south of the trackway, is a reminder of the importance of the route. The first documentary references come from Saxon times, when it was described as the 'herepath' in charters relating to Fovant and Swallowcliffe, and as 'the broad highway' in an Ebbesbourne charter.

Throughout the medieval period the Salisbury Way continued in existence as the main route from Salisbury to the west, and it was almost certainly used by pilgrims travelling to Wilton and Shaftesbury Abbeys, and by longer-distance travellers on horseback. Later, during the coaching era, it was improved to form 14 miles of the Exeter Road from London through Salisbury and Shaftesbury to the west.

The ancient trackway suffered from two severe disadvantages as a coach route: the upland way was remote from shelter and exposed to the elements, and at each end a steep hill had to be negotiated. But the valley alternative was even worse. Even in 1830 the roads here were described as 'impassable for any other four-wheeled carriages than those used for husbandry purposes, and suited only for a sure-footed horse'. Difficult as they undoubtedly were, the ascents of Whitesheet Hill and Harnham Hill were preferable to the heavy lowland clays, especially in winter.

Improved road-making techniques in the nineteenth century at last made a route along the Nadder valley a feasible proposition and incidentally spelt the end of the Salisbury Way as a through route. As late as 1791 the valley road is omitted from a map of the area, but it must have been built very soon thereafter. The new road diverged from the old at the foot of Whitesheet Hill, linked the valley settlements of Swallowcliffe, Fovant and Barford St Martin, and at last avoided the difficult gradients of Whitesheet and Harnham. The Salisbury Way was reduced to a track used by local farmers, and has changed very little since.

The new valley road had not existed long before another competitor for long-distance travellers appeared. In 1859 the railway was extended westwards from Salisbury to Tisbury and Yeovil, destroying the coach trade along the new road. The Glove Inn, at the foot of Whitesheet Hill, had survived the demise of the Salisbury Way, but now became one of the many casualties as the traffic dried up; the buildings now form part of Arundell Farm. And on the old ridge route, as Desmond Hawkins has said, 'grass softened and covered the wheel ruts . . . what was once a major coach route is now a deserted grassy track.'

Description of the Route

The Salisbury Way diverges from the A30 as a muddy track passing to the right of a row of houses (ST933239) opposite the minor road leading to Sands Farm (Arundell Farm, ¼ mile to the west was, as we have seen, the Glove Inn, the staging post for the London coach, but is now reduced to a nondescript collection of buildings). The track quickly swings left and begins to climb steadily, its surface betraying the remains of recent metalling and also bearing signs of fairly regular use by agricultural vehicles.

Thankfully the busy A30 is soon out of earshot, and the ascent of Whitesheet Hill – actually an easy task, involving a climb of only about 300ft – begins in earnest. The Salisbury Way is sometimes enclosed in a cutting during the climb, but in places there is a wide view to the left over the well-wooded Nadder valley.

The summit of Whitesheet Hill is marked by an OS triangulation pillar in a field just to the left of the track; the height is 242m (794ft), the highest point attained on the walk. A hundred yards to the west, however, is a long barrow,

(*opposite*) The tree-fringed course of Salisbury Way as it passes Wilton hare warren

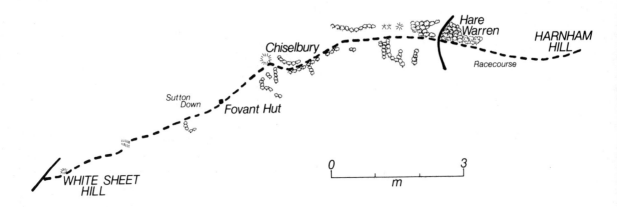

protected by barbed wire but accessible over a thoughtfully provided stile. Near the summit a milestone was erected in 1796 to inform coach travellers that Salisbury was now 14 miles distant, and London's Hyde Park Corner a daunting 97 miles.

The Salisbury Way curves slightly left after passing the OS pillar, and the next mile or so of the route is revealed as a green lane marching directly along the ridge between barbed wire fences, with only a few hawthorn bushes for company. After a while the views northward over the Nadder valley are complemented by views to the south, where the Ebble valley is backed by the low hills of Cranborne Chase. In the foreground an enormous field takes up most of Gallows Hill; when freshly ploughed the ground appears to be lightly covered with snow, so prominent are the gleaming chalky stones.

A copse to the north of the green lane marks the crossing of the Alvediston to Ansty road, one of only two to brave the scarp overlooking the Nadder valley. The road plunges down by means of a hairpin bend, then crosses the A30 to arrive at Ansty, an attractive village almost worth the detour for the

Salisbury Way on the summit of Whitesheet Hill, looking west towards Shaftesbury

The village pond at Ansty

sight of its 72ft maypole, the highest in England, next to the village pond. The Maypole Inn, a useful lunchtime port of call, was formerly the Arundell Arms, taking its name from the family at the 'big house', for Ansty was an estate village of Wardour Castle.

Back on the ridge, the Salisbury Way heads across Swallowcliffe Down, with the site of an Iron Age settlement just south of the way, to the Fovant Hut, once a refreshment stop for the London coaches (the Compton Hut, which served a similar purpose, has not survived). Across the second road, this time linking Fovant with the tiny hamlet of Fifield Bavant, the green lane continues along the crest of Fovant Down. Below the crest are a series of regimental badges and sundry other decorations, the first of them carved into the chalk by Australian soldiers during World War I.

On top of the ridge are the grassy banks and ditches of Chiselbury Camp, an Iron Age fortress spectacularly sited where the chalk ridge thrusts out into the valley. The Salisbury Way curves right here along Compton Down, its course unfolding, in Timperley and Brill's words, 'like an uncurled snake across the light greens and buffs of the downland fields on either side'. The richly wooded setting of places like Fovant (an attractive village of stone cottages and watercress beds) and Compton Chamberlayne contrasts vividly with the stark simplicity of the upland landscape through which the Salisbury Way slowly descends to the Wilton hare warren.

East of the hare warren and Neale's Barrow, a tumulus hidden in the woods, the ancient trackway and later coach route now merges with the access road to Salisbury Racecourse, whose grandstand appears especially incongruous after the long miles of solitude on the Salisbury Way. Yet the entire 14 mile length of the way formed the course for a race instituted by the Earl of Pembroke in the sixteenth century. There was a second course, from North Down Farm in Broad Chalke to the hare warren, which was about 4 miles in length, and legend has it that Sir Thomas Thynne's horse, Peacock, ran this course in five minutes – a literally incredible feat, since he would have been travelling much faster than an Epsom Derby winner!

The way is now only a mile from Harnham Hill and the descent into Salisbury, down the Old Blandford Road – close to the site of an Iron Age village and a Saxon cemetery – and across Ayleswade Bridge. Built by Bishop Bingham in 1244 to divert traffic from Wilton and Old Sarum to the new town at Salisbury, the bridge crosses the River Avon and an artificial channel, with the former chapel of St John (now a private house) on the island between them. To the north of the bridge are St Nicholas' Hospital, founded by Bishop Poore in the thirteenth century, and the flimsy remains of De Vaux College, dating from 1261 and regarded by some authorities as the earliest university college in England.

Bear left now, through Harnham Gate and into the walled Cathedral Close and, finally, Salisbury Cathedral itself (SU143295). A creation of the thirteenth century, when Salisbury was founded to replace the hilltop city of Old Sarum, which was regarded by then as *ventis expositus, sterilis, aridus, desertus* (exposed to the winds, sterile, arid, deserted), the cathedral can boast the tallest spire in Britain (404ft) and a classically unified Early English appearance. It is a superb final objective for the Salisbury Way.

Notes

Map OS 1:50,000 sheet 184.
Further reading H. M. Timperley and Edith Brill, *Ancient Trackways of Wessex* (Shipston-on-Stour: Drinkwater, 2nd edn. 1983); Desmond Hawkins, *Cranborne Chase* (Gollancz, 1980).
Public transport The Salisbury to Shaftesbury bus service (quite frequent on weekdays) calls at Birdbush, Ludwell (1 mile west of Sands Farm). Salisbury station has rail services to London Waterloo, Southampton, Bristol and the west of England.

46

8

ACKLING DYKE

Stratford Tony to Badbury Rings 16 miles/26km

Ackling Dyke, from Old Sarum to Badbury Rings in Dorset, formed part of the Roman road from London to the south-west. The walk from Vernditch Chase to Badbury Rings includes some of the most spectacular Roman earthworks in the country, and since only short sections are followed by modern roads it is an outstanding 'Roman' walk.

Historical Background

The main Roman artery linking London and south-west England passed through Silchester, Old Sarum (the former site of Salisbury), the Iron Age encampment at Badbury Rings, and Dorchester, on its way to Exeter. Parts of it are now known by different names, and they have suffered widely differing fates. West of Silchester the road, known as the Port Way, has largely been abandoned, although as it approaches Old Sarum it reappears as a long straight country lane. Between Old Sarum and Badbury Rings Ackling Dyke, as the Roman road is now called, is mostly ignored by modern roads and there are substantial sections of footpath on the well-preserved agger (embankment) as it traverses Cranborne Chase.

The Roman road-makers showed a fine disregard for earlier earthworks, cutting through the Dorset Cursus – an extraordinary prehistoric monument consisting of parallel earthworks 6 miles long – on Bottlebush Down and also passing through Grim's Ditch and other defensive earthworks. But Ackling Dyke was later to suffer the same fate: in the fourth century AD, as Roman power weakened and rebellions closer to the heart of the Empire claimed more attention, Bokerley Ditch was constructed by the local people to protect their settlements from attack, and the new dyke blocked the old Roman road at Bokerley Junction.

Cranborne Chase, though quite heavily settled, seems to have offered little threat to the Romans and the road was not defended by forts; indeed, the native settlements at Woodcuts and Rotherley continued in existence, and Romano-British settlements grew up at Woodyates and Badbury Rings. Conversely, few Roman villa sites have been found on the Chase, and it appears to have been a region of passage rather than exploitation.

47

Description of the Route

The Roman road leading south-west from Old Sarum is difficult to follow on the ground for the first few miles, and a sensible alternative is to start at Stratford Tony (SU093263), a village named, appropriately enough, from the 'street ford' where the Romans negotiated the River Ebble. One of the innumerable small villages in this part of the world which are remarkably attractive yet are missed by the guidebooks, Stratford Tony has a church with a Perpendicular tower, a Georgian manor house, the thatched Lavender

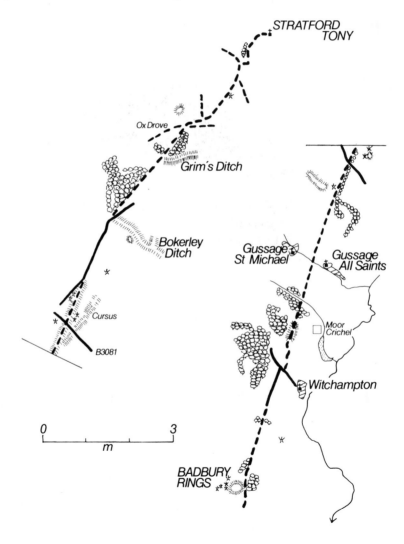

The Icknield Way below Crowell Hill

Cottage and some pleasant houses fronting on to a modern ford across the Ebble.

The way out of the little village lies past the church and along a lane to Throope Farm, then uphill, somewhat to the east of the Roman alignment for a while, before rejoining it at grid reference 081253, as it begins to climb towards a tumulus on the flat summit of Faulston Down. Beyond the flat summit the path is clearly seen to be sited upon the agger of the Roman road; here there is a distinct westward shift in its direction, then another to the south to resume the original alignment from Old Sarum.

Just before Knighton Wood is reached, the road intersects the Ox Drove, one of the classic east–west prehistoric ridgeways of south Wiltshire (see the Salisbury Way chapter for more details). The Ox Drove can be thoroughly recommended as a walk, from Win Green, the highest point on Cranborne Chase, eastwards past the Iron Age hill-fort on Winklebury Hill and along green lanes to Woodminton Down and Coombe Bissett.

A track, again on the agger, now leads past the western edge of Knighton Wood, with Grim's Ditch in close attendance at its southern end. The next part of the walk is extremely enjoyable, on a narrow footpath between thick hedges but with frequent glimpses of the rolling downland of Cranborne Chase on either side. The hedges, and indeed the path itself, are overgrown with creeping ivy, but beneath it can be seen the agger, raised possibly two or three feet above the surrounding land. The path crosses a minor road and then keeps to the left-hand margin of the Forestry Commission's Vernditch Chase plantation as a rutted cart-track.

Ackling Dyke, still impressively raised above the fields it crosses, now intersects with the A354 at Bokerley Junction. The last hundred yards are heavily overgrown with blackberries, nettles and assorted bushes. It is well worth while devoting some time to an exploration of Bokerley Ditch, the massive rampart on the far side of the main road. It seems to have been constructed early in the fourth century AD, to block attempts to penetrate Cranborne Chase from the north; the dyke extends for some four miles and originally adjoined thick woodland at each end. Bokerley Ditch was twice repaired, after rebellions against the weakening Roman regime, in 367 (when it was extended to block Ackling Dyke) and again at the beginning of the fifth century.

South of Bokerley Junction is Woodyates, the site of a Romano-British settlement and much more recently of a coaching inn once owned by Robert Browning, great-grandfather of the poet, and used as a setting by Thomas Hardy in *Crusted Characters*. The inn, latterly known as the Shaftesbury

The view west along the Salisbury Way from the summit of Whitesheet Hill

The overgrown footpath following the agger of Ackling Dyke on Vernditch Chase

Arms, was described by Treves in 1906, in *Highways and Byways in Dorset*, as deplorably modernised and badly run, but Hardy commented on its 'genial hostelry appearance'. Now the site is occupied by bungalows, which together with a few council houses and some farm buildings comprise the unremarkable present-day settlement.

Ackling Dyke coincides with the A354 for about a mile, at the end of which the road bears right and its Roman predecessor can clearly be seen crossing open countryside to the left of a number of prominent round barrows. As Margary says,

> It is impossible to exaggerate, and indeed difficult adequately to describe, the magnificence which now lies ahead. For mile after mile, up hill and down, practically all the way to Badbury Rings, the road is seen (and well seen, for much of it is on open downland) as an enormous agger, over 40 feet wide, sometimes 50 feet, and high in proportion, often 4–5 or even over 6 feet high.

Perhaps the best spot from which to appreciate this extraordinary sight is Bottlebush Down, where the road from Sixpenny Handley to Cranborne crosses Ackling Dyke. The northern panorama, with the grassy banks of the Roman road spearing between ploughed fields and the wooded remnants of the Chase on the skyline, will not easily be forgotten. And to the south the Dyke continues as a major landscape feature, with the path following the crest of the earthwork.

Yet, despite the excellence of the Roman road, of Bokerley Ditch, and of the burial mounds and other prehistoric remains, the most remarkable exhibit of this treasurehouse of antiquity is still to be discussed. This is the Dorset Cursus, a 6 mile long prehistoric monument consisting of parallel banks about a hundred yards apart and incorporating various tumuli in its course. The cursus, whose purpose is just as obscure as that of Silbury Hill, near Avebury, extends from near Pentridge to Thickthorn Down, but it is at its most visible, impressive and tantalising on Bottlebush Down.

Badbury Rings is still about 8 miles distant, but the way towards it is so straight and undemanding that it is easily reached. Gradually the agger becomes less marked, and by the time the lane linking two of the three Gussages (St Michael and All Saints) is reached, Ackling Dyke, well signposted as such, has become a wide, dusty field road. Gussage St Michael has a simple flint church with a medieval ladder staircase to the belfry and a Victorian rood screen; All Saints, a pleasant and quiet hamlet occupied by farmers and metalworkers in pre-Roman times, has a Georgian manor house and flint-banded church tower.

The field road from the north becomes a footpath running between hedges across the quarried hillocks on Sovell Down. Where the path meets another country lane it is worth walking a few yards east along this to see the agger of Ackling Dyke descending the hillside. Next, a path signposted to Holly Copse marks the route along the edge of a field towards woods.

Just before it reaches the eastern outliers of the hamlet of Manswood, Ackling Dyke becomes a surfaced lane, but after crossing the minor road here it reverts to a bridleway (signposted to Sheephouse), losing the direct line for a while as it passes a curiously turreted country house. At Sheephouse the agger has all but disappeared. To the left here is Moor Crichel and Crichel Park, too much of a detour at this stage. The Roman road is taken over by a very minor country lane, pretty well free of traffic, and south of a crossroads it exists today as a lane serving Bradford Farm, near which it goes right, signposted to Badbury. This is a muddy cart-track skirting large fields at first, but after a minor stream it becomes a narrow path heading directly for Badbury Rings, which begins to dominate the southerly prospect.

Badbury Rings (ST964030), which the Roman road by-passes immediately

(*left*) Ackling Dyke at its most impressive on Bottlebush Down; (*right*) The northern entrance to the Iron Age hill-fort of Badbury Rings

to the east, is a huge and impressive multivallate hill-fort crowning a minor chalk hill, which the Romans clearly used as a focus for their road system – Ackling Dyke passes through from north-east to south-west, and other roads went north-west towards Shaftesbury and south to Poole harbour. There are three concentric banks and ditches, with a wooded enclosed area at the top of the hill. Currently the National Trust is re-seeding areas which have been badly eroded (there is a large car park and the area is extremely popular at weekends), but the high barbed-wire fence barricading off the whole of the hill-fort seems a draconian measure out of sympathy with the superb setting of this historic site.

Notes

Maps   OS 1:50,000 sheets 184 and 195.
Further reading   Desmond Hawkins, *Cranborne Chase* (Gollancz, 1980); Denys Kay-Robinson, *The Landscape of Thomas Hardy* (Webb & Bower, 1984); Ivan Margary, *Roman Roads in Britain* (John Baker, 3rd edn. 1973).
Accommodation   Plentiful in Salisbury and adequate in Wimborne Minster, but virtually non-existent closer to the start and finish of the walk.
Public transport   There are regular but not especially frequent bus services (best on Tuesdays, Thursdays and Saturdays) between Salisbury and Coombe Bissett, 1 mile from Stratford Tony; these services also call at Woodyates. Badbury Rings has two services on Fridays only from Wimborne Minster. Wimborne has a half-hourly service to Poole.

9

THE MARINERS WAY

Sticklepath to Widecombe in the Moor 13 miles/21km

The Mariners Way across Devon is not a single trackway in its own right but was created by sailors travelling between the ports of Bideford and Dartmouth, who linked existing lanes, tracks and footpaths to form a direct route. The most interesting section, especially for walkers, uses paths and country lanes skirting the eastern fringe of Dartmoor.

Historical Background

Elements of the Mariners Way have no doubt existed since prehistoric times, when the moorland itself was surprisingly heavily settled; other parts date from the Saxon settlement of the Dartmoor fringes; but the way was not formalised as a through route until much later, with the growth of Bideford and Dartmouth in medieval times and the need for sailors to journey from one to the other in search of work. Indeed, the Mariners Way reached the peak of its popularity as late as the eighteenth century.

The manner in which the Mariners Way evolved, by linking pre-existing tracks, has inevitably given rise to speculation that it was not a true long-distance path at all. Indeed, William Crossing says that, 'I have heard it spoken of as being merely a way from Zeal to Widecombe church'; but he concludes that 'there is good reason for believing that it extended right across the county'. He suggests that there were rest-houses every 8 or 10 miles along the way, though little evidence of this now survives. Entries in the Gidleigh church records between 1730 and 1774 record the giving of alms to sailors, and this both supports the tradition that the route existed and also emphasises the historical period during which it was most heavily used.

The way can only be traced with any certainty in its central section, as it skirts the eastern fringe of Dartmoor. It seems to have linked Bideford and Great Torrington via the Torridge valley and then to have made for South Zeal. From here, lanes and paths mark the route through Throwleigh, Gidleigh, Glassy Steps and Yardworthy to Lettaford. The Mariners Way then avoided the crest of Hamel Down, keeping to its eastern slopes through Combe, Hookney and Widecombe. The way south to Dartmouth is uncertain but it probably went via Ashburton and Totnes.

55

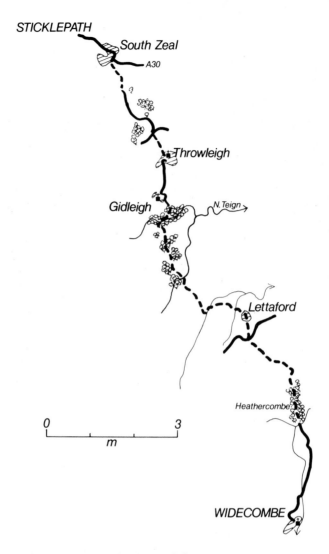

Description of the Route

Start at Sticklepath (SX641941), notable for three things: the spring water of the Lady Well, close to the Mariners Way and no doubt a source of refreshment, especially for the packhorses, in the eighteenth century; the Quaker graveyard close to the River Taw; and the museum of industrial archaeology, housed in the former Finch Brothers' foundry. Once a corn mill, later a cloth mill, it became a precision tool factory in 1814, producing agricultural implements in addition to custom-made tools for the china-clay industry.

The old Exeter to Okehampton road passed through Zeal Head and South Zeal, and this is the way to go to escape the noisome A30. South Zeal is a former borough (the old burgage tenements are shown on the Outdoor

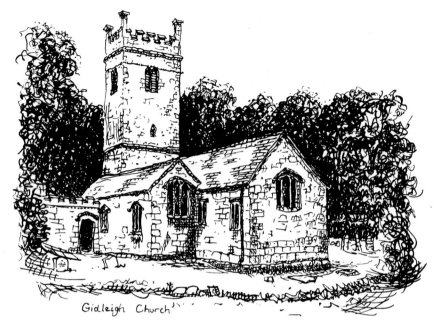

Gidleigh Church

Leisure map) and was at its most prosperous in the coaching days; it now has an air of slightly surprised tranquillity. Climb steeply out of the east end of the village, then turn right and almost immediately fork right again along a lane leading to the A30. Go straight across (with extreme care) on to a lane heading south to Ramsley Farm and the Domesday manor of West Wyke, now represented by a building dating from 1656.

The narrow lane continues south to join the road leading along the moorland edge to Clannaborough. Shortly after this, take the footpath on the right, crossing a series of fields to the churchyard at Throwleigh, a delightful and rewarding Dartmoor hamlet, full of totally unspoilt cottages. The church is fifteenth century, with a priest's doorway and a pulpit composed of fragments of the medieval rood screen. Across the churchyard from the path bearing the Mariners Way is the Tudor church house, next to the lych-gate, and up the hill a little is a cottage with a granite exterior staircase.

The Mariners Way leaves the churchyard through a small gate, descends a flight of steps to a little lane (there is a signpost here), then cuts straight across the lane to continue as a narrow and overgrown footpath. This quickly improves, however, and enters the hamlet of Forder as Deave Lane, a classic unsurfaced Devon lane worn to the bedrock in places and hemmed in by trees on both sides.

Turn right out of Deave Lane, then left twice in the space of fifty yards to follow a narrow lane, fortunately almost traffic-free, past Chapple Farm to Gidleigh, the second fascinating hamlet encountered on this walk. The ruins of Gidleigh Castle, actually no more than a fortified manor house, are private,

Cottages at Throwleigh

The stony, tree-lined Deave Lane
near Forder

but the granite church, complete with a fine Tudor rood screen and a brook running through the churchyard, is worth a visit. There is also a small youth hostel next to the church.

South from Gidleigh the road reaches a T-junction. Turn right, then after 200 yards take the track on the left (again signposted as the Mariners Way, and now waymarked with yellow splashes). The track, somewhat muddy in places, leads between an old, varied hedgerow on the left and a forestry plantation, fronted by bracken and blackberries, on the right. Beyond a gate bear slightly right (yellow indicates the way) into a pine glade, then through bracken and finally through the trees again, going much more steeply downhill now, on a slippery, rocky path.

The river – the North Teign – can be heard below and the path appears to be making straight for it, but at the last moment it emerges from the trees and swings sharply right, heading up the north bank of the river before dropping down to cross it on a modern footbridge – the successor to the much less secure Glassy Steps. Now the way lies uphill, still waymarked, to the cluster of houses at Teigncombe.

For the next mile or so the route coincides with the Two Moors Way, an unofficial long-distance route. The way lies south, skirting Kes Tor with its prehistoric hut circles and natural rock basin, to Frenchbeer, Teignworthy and Yardworthy. At Yardworthy the remains of a moorland farmhouse of the fourteenth century – possibly the oldest surviving domestic building on Dartmoor – can be seen. Next, after the Two Moors Way diverges to cross Chagford Common, are Shapley, another hamlet mentioned in Domesday Book, and the farms of Hurston, Lingcombe and Jurston.

At Jurston the Mariners Way, now a well-defined track, is again signposted as such as it crosses the moor-edge road linking Chagford and Princetown. Between Hurston and the superb little hamlet of Lettaford it is specifically marked on the OS map as an ancient trackway, and it rises to the occasion, first as a wide, gritty lane between tall hedges and then, entering Lettaford, as a slightly sunken way worn to the bare rock by centuries of continuous use. Lettaford, aloof from the busy B3212, is comparatively unknown, a straggling collection of houses at the end of a narrow lane, yet is of timeless beauty and possesses an early-seventeenth-century longhouse – complete with peacock.

The way out of Lettaford is not quite as shown on the Outdoor Leisure map. Instead of bearing right, in front of a row of cottages, keep straight on – signposted Mariners Way – through a farmyard and then bear slightly right to join the path leading to Leapra Cross and the B3212. Continue straight ahead, to Moor Gate and West Combe, where William Crossing reports the way as having run through the passage of a dwelling, presumably one which offered accommodation to weary mariners.

Now the links with the moor become a little tenuous for a while as the path follows a lowland route across the fields to Lower Hookner, Kendon and Heathercombe. From the last named a highly interesting expedition can be undertaken across Hamel Down to Grimspound, a Bronze Age village with twenty-four hut sites enclosed by a partly rebuilt drystone wall. One of the largest of the many prehistoric pounds on Dartmoor, Grimspound is by no means representative of them but serves to illustrate the capacity for organisation of prehistoric man.

The enclosing wall of Grimspound is a massive 9ft thick and about 5ft high, with a paved passageway forming the main entrance through the wall. The settlement could not easily be defended and this, together with the presence of a little brook running through the pound, suggests Grimspound was built by farmers to water and protect their livestock.

The end of the walk at Widecombe in the Moor is only 2 miles or so from Heathercombe, though sadly part of this distance is taken up with road walking. First, though, there is a short walk through woodland; at the road, turn right, passing the entrance to Natsworthy Manor (the highest Domesday manor in Devon), then use a useful short-cut footpath where the road curves round to Ley Farm. Now keep to the road as it follows the wooded valley of the East Webburn river down between Hamel Down and Chinkwell Tor to enter the tourist honeypot of Widecombe (SX718767).

Widecombe is best seen out of season and on a weekday, though it can absorb remarkable numbers of visitors – as I discovered on ending this walk there on August Bank Holiday Monday. Easily the most commercially developed of Dartmoor's villages, it is probably best known for its fair, described in the *National Park Guide* as 'of no great antiquity and . . . quite alien to the nature and spirit of Dartmoor'. More interesting are the fourteenth-century parish church, known as 'the cathedral of the moor', the National Trust's Church House and the late medieval Glebe House.

Notes

Maps OS 1:25,000 Outdoor Leisure sheet 28 (Dartmoor), or 1:50,000 sheet 191.
Further reading S. H. Burton, *Devon Villages* (Robert Hale, 1973); William Crossing, *Guide to Dartmoor* (David & Charles, new edn. 1965); W. G. Hoskins, *Devon* (David & Charles, 1954).
Public transport With care a day's walk can be arranged using buses to and from Exeter. Sticklepath is served by the Exeter to Okehampton bus service (approximately hourly), whilst Widecombe has a limited service, on Wednesdays only except in July and August, to Ashburton (connections to Plymouth, Newton Abbot and Exeter).

10

THE ABBOT'S WAY

Buckfast Abbey to Princetown 12 miles/19km

Whilst the genesis of the Abbot's Way is shrouded in uncertainty – and undoubtedly its claim to monastic origins is not strictly accurate – the scenic merits of the walk are incontestable. This is one of the classic walks of southern Britain, striking across Dartmoor to Princetown and passing on the way prehistoric remains, medieval crosses and a modern reservoir. It demands respect in mist and can be marshy in places after heavy rain, but it is otherwise easy to follow and repays the effort handsomely.

Historical Background

It is all too easy to classify the Abbot's Way as an early medieval track trodden into existence by the monks of Buckfast Abbey on their way to Tavistock or Buckland Abbeys. But we have already seen that most ancient trackways have a far more complex history than that, and that religious labels – the Pilgrims' Way, for instance – can be misleading. This is the case with the Abbot's Way, too: and not only does the track pre-date the monks, even the crosses which might be expected to provide conclusive proof of monastic travel are not what they seem to be.

Southern Dartmoor was a hive of prehistoric activity, and the map is thick with indications of settlement sites, cattle pounds and burial chambers. The circular boundary walls of Bronze Age settlements can be picked out on Dean Moor, close to cairn circles and tumuli; at Erme Pound, just south of the Abbot's Way, is a fine example of a Dartmoor cattle enclosure; and further west an extraordinary stone row crosses the path. Indeed, cairns and the like keep the Abbot's Way close company, yet it is not certain that the track was in use as a through route during this period. It may have been, but the distribution of prehistoric settlements on Dartmoor suggests a southern origin for the settlers, who may have used the river valleys for communication.

So the early medieval monks may have linked a series of different tracks, converting them for their own use. They may, too, have erected crosses to mark the way, though not all of the Abbot's Way crosses can be accounted for in this way, since Nun's Cross (previously known as Siward's Cross) was well known before 1280, when Buckland Abbey was granted adjacent lands

61

Nun's Cross

at Walkhampton. Another puzzle is the *lack* of crosses along the way (apart from Nun's Cross there is only Huntingdon Cross) compared with the more direct route between Buckfast and Tavistock, over Holne Ridge, which is peppered with crosses on Ter Hill. Despite the uncertainties, however, the route was certainly used by monks (and also by others needing to cross the moor, whether on foot, on horseback or with packhorse trains) during the Middle Ages, so that its popular name is not entirely undeserved.

Description of the Route

The village of Buckfast, at the start of the walk (SX741674), has been eclipsed by its daughter settlement to the south, Buckfastleigh, which has grown into a small town, but Buckfast remains better known because of Buckfast Abbey, a modern building but a focus of interest for pilgrims and for more mundane tourists. Founded by the Benedictines in about 1030 and later endowed by King Canute, its fortunes declined rapidly until 1134, when it was re-founded by the monks of Savigny and became Cistercian.

After the Dissolution Buckfast Abbey was allowed to become ruinous, and it was only in 1882, when the property was bought by a community of French Benedictines, that its revival began. The monks began the reconstruction of the Abbey in 1907, opened the church in 1932 and completed the tower in 1938. The building, which incorporates some earlier features such as the Abbot's Tower, is architecturally unexceptional. Close by, on the

River Dart, is Higher Buckfast Mill, a reminder of the days when Buckfast-leigh was a thriving wool town.

The first section of the walk lies along the road west from Buckfast, through suburban sprawl and then the more tranquil surroundings of Hockmoor to Cross Furzes, formerly a more important road junction on the edge of the moor. The road ends here, but a rough, stony track marked Abbot's Way goes quite steeply down, accompanied on the left by a tall hedge, to a little wood. On the way down the network of fields on the lower slopes of Dartmoor can be seen ahead – though as the walk progresses these soon give way to the barren wastes more characteristic of the Abbot's Way.

The path through the wood crosses Dean Burn on a superb clapper bridge fashioned from massive slate slabs and shaded by ancient trees, then rises sharply, leaves the wood and crosses the first of several fields. The route is very clear indeed – if anything it is too well waymarked, with frequent posts bedecked with blue streaks of paint. Beyond a stile the route dips to cross a small stream (look back east here to the rocky horizon of the Haytor hills) then rises again through rough pasture to reach the gate giving access on to the open moor at Water Oak Corner. Once through the gate the walker is increasingly committed to crossing the moor: in mist or worsening weather, a return to Buckfast is the sensible course of action.

The path westwards from the battered trees at Water Oak Corner is not immediately obvious, but after slanting up slightly to the right for about a hundred yards it can be picked out ahead through the rough grazing. After

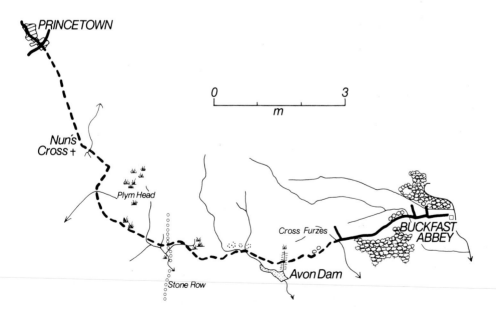

five minutes or so, by which time the path is well established, a spiky guide-post is found, at the top of a slope overlooking the Avon Dam Reservoir.

The Abbot's Way drops down the slope, fords a stream and curves round to the north of the reservoir, past the low walls of Bronze Age settlements, probably best seen in winter, when the bracken is at its least obstructive. The path often takes the form of a stony, sunken trackway as it approaches Bishop's Meads, with the infant River Avon down on the left and another settlement with its circular boundary wall high on the right.

Now the path fords the surprisingly wide Western Wella Brook and passes Huntingdon Cross, a stubby, solid guide-post in the wild Avon valley, and apparently a meeting-place for the black cattle of the area. To the west of Huntingdon Cross the Abbot's Way fords the Avon (another clapper bridge, a little further upstream, is an alternative after rain) and continues across the sombre and often featureless moor until it crosses the remains of the tramway which used to serve the Red Lake china-clay works. The spoil-heaps and flooded pits lie ½ mile to the north. Red Lake ford and the surrounding marsh have to be negotiated carefully, and then the intermittent path passes through the longest stone row in Dartmoor, which extends for over 2 miles in the upper Erme valley.

Now comes the crucial test in route-finding, as the Abbot's Way reaches Erme Head, crosses into the Plym valley and fords the river only ½ mile from its source, and rises again to the west of Crane Hill to make for Nun's Cross (the way to Buckland diverges at Broad Rock, heading down the Plym valley and across Gutter Tor). In fine weather the route should be obvious, but in mist it is all too easy to be led astray.

The way curves round to the west of Great Gnats' Head, slants down to Plym Ford, passes more derelict tin workings and then bears north-east across the gently undulating slopes of Crane Hill. Further north-east is Childe's Tomb, described by the OS as a 'cross on cairn or cist', and possibly commemorating a Devonian giant of the tenth century. But the Abbot's Way turns north-west again, descending from the high moor to Nun's Cross Ford in the Swincombe valley, and then to Nun's Cross Farm.

The farm, in its exposed and isolated position some 1,300ft above sea-level, was enclosed by Richard Hooper in the 1870s. He built a small, low farmhouse which within a few decades became ruinous; it still stands, however, and has undergone considerable repairs, but it is no longer the centre of a farm holding. The turf and granite block walls of the fields surrounding the farm can still be traced, together with primitive drainage

(*opposite top*) The clapper bridge carrying Abbot's Way over the Dean Burn; (*bottom*) Huntingdon Cross and the Avon valley

channels. A more formidable water channel contours the hillside to the north-east, serving the former Whiteworks tin mine.

The Abbot's Way continues north-west for 200 yards or so to Nun's Cross, originally known as Siward's Cross. The tall granite cross, desecrated in the nineteenth century and hence held together by iron struts at mid-height, was mentioned in a thirteenth-century document and, standing at an important junction of moorland tracks, was probably always a forest boundary marker and guide-post. From the cross take the more easterly of the two marked paths leading north, and traverse a level, barren landscape of rocks, rough pasture and a little heather. The way passes a few boundary stones before scaling South Hessary Tor, a particularly attractive rock outcrop overlooking the rather less attractive sprawl of Princetown.

From South Hessary Tor the path, enclosed between stone walls, descends from the moor straight into the centre of Princetown, conveniently close to the excellent Plume of Feathers Inn (SX591735). This is an extraordinary site for a town, at 1,400ft in the middle of Dartmoor, blessed by more than its fair share of snow, wind and rain. But it was close to Sir Thomas Tyrwhitt's granite quarries and to his estate at Tor Royal, reclaimed from the moor from 1780 onwards. Tyrwhitt was also instrumental in the building of the prison here. Originally constructed to house prisoners during the Napoleonic Wars, it was opened in 1806, at a cost of £130,000, and held up to 9,000 prisoners.

The prison closed in 1816, but was reopened in 1850 for long-term prisoners and it has been considerably extended since. In a macabre way it has even become a tourist attraction, with lay-bys provided at a suitable spot on the B3212. The town, named after the Prince of Wales, whose Duchy of Cornwall owned the land, is universally dismissed as 'grim' but is a fine centre for exploring south-western Dartmoor in addition to the Abbot's Way.

Notes

Maps OS 1:25,000 Outdoor Leisure sheet 28 (Dartmoor), or 1:50,000 sheets 191 and 202.
Further reading Countryside Commission, *Dartmoor National Park*, (HMSO, 1969); J. H. B. Peel, *Along the Green Roads of Britain* (repub. David & Charles, 1982); R. Hansford Worth, *Dartmoor* (new edn., ed. Spooner & Russell, David & Charles, 1967).
Public transport Buckfast Abbey has an approximately hourly bus service from Newton Abbot and Ashburton, and five buses a day from Plymouth. Princetown has only a summer service from Plymouth – two buses a day on Sundays and Wednesdays (daily in August).

Huntingdon Cross and the upper Avon valley, on the Abbot's Way across Dartmoor

11

THE EXMOOR RIDGEWAY

Wheddon Cross to Chapman Barrows 16 miles/26km

This walk along the crest of the Exmoor hills is a comparatively challenging expedition; the walker starts with the long pull up to Dunkery Beacon, then encounters route-finding problems in the middle of the moorland plateau and finally faces a damp crossing of the Chains. The rewards include long views across the National Park to the North Devon coast – and, on clear days, across the Bristol Channel to the Welsh hills – together with a series of visits to important and attractive archaeological sites.

Historical Background

Whilst there is inevitably no definite proof of its use in prehistoric times, circumstantial evidence points to the Exmoor Ridgeway as one of the first roads in Britain – contemporary with the Kerry Hills ridgeway as a Bronze Age trackway across a remote upland. The trackway ran across the crest of the Brendon Hills, climbed up on to the southern shoulder of Dunkery Beacon, crossed Exe Plain and the Chains, and reached the coast at Morte Point by way of Blackmoor Gate. Evidence for its Bronze Age origins lies in the remarkable collection of burial mounds, standing stones and even stone rows and circles which line its route.

The Exmoor Ridgeway was also known to and utilised by the Saxon invaders in the seventh century, although they also created new, lower routes such as the 'herepath' or military road branching from the Brendon Hills ridgeway just to the east of Wheddon Cross and running past Horsecombe towards Exford. In general their settlements, too, kept to the lower slopes, although the placenames of Pinkworthy and Radworthy, the latter now deserted though still flourishing in the seventeenth century, indicate Saxon colonisation of the moorland edge.

After the Norman conquest the heart of Exmoor became a royal forest – not, though, a tract of woodland but a game preserve which remained unchanged and uncultivated throughout the Middle Ages. Only when John Knight acquired the whole of the former royal hunting ground in the early

The Fosse Way crossing the Avon valley near Malmesbury, Wiltshire

69

nineteenth century were attempts made to impose man's agricultural will on the high moorland. The results of Knight's enterprise were decidedly mixed, but one remaining monument is the forest wall enclosing his estate, which he had all but completed in 1824. Part of this wall, along the South Chains, used the route of the ancient ridgeway.

Knight attempted to drain the high moorland plateau around the Chains, but to no avail: he was unable to crack the 'iron pan', which artificially raised the water table and led to waterlogging and the extensive and unpleasant bog, mostly nourishing only deer sedge, which survives today. Only the rough remains of the failed drainage ditches (some of them a danger to the unsuspecting walker) are left today in this desolate area, neglected yet nevertheless evocative of the true spirit of Exmoor.

Description of the Route

Start the walk at Wheddon Cross (SS924387), where the Brendon Hills ridgeway, now a minor road offering an exhilarating drive, briefly descends from the heights: its westerly extension is the Exmoor Ridgeway. This is represented initially by the road past Combeshead to Dunkery Gate, but it is usually awash with tourist traffic in the summer and there is another route to Dunkery Gate which, whilst historically less accurate, is much to be preferred. This route is the footpath leading past Watercombe and then alongside the wooded and very attractive Mansley Combe, eventually ascending close to marvellous waterfalls (sometimes devoid of water in

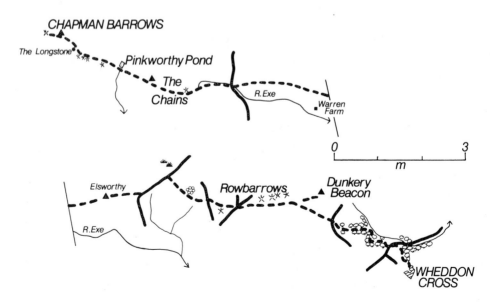

(left) The dry waterfall in Mansley Combe; (right) The summit of Dunkery Beacon

summer and therefore offering scramblers an exciting alternative) to reach Dunkery Gate.

Cross the recently renewed bridge here and select a track on the far side of the road: either the ridgeway, straight across the heathery plateau, with Dunkery Beacon on the right, or one of the paths leading up to the summit of the Beacon, which is easily conquered, pleasantly rocky but normally very crowded. On a clear day (which I have yet to experience here) the view is reputed to be both extremely impressive, especially along the northern face of the Exmoor hills, and very extensive. The Beacon itself, at 1,706ft (520m) the highest point of Exmoor, was used as a signal-station in late medieval times.

Beyond the burial mounds known as the Rowbarrows, due west from Dunkery Beacon, lies the crest of the Exmoor ridge and the plateau known as the Chains, terminating at Chapman Barrows – fittingly also the terminus of this walk. Start towards them down the gently sloping western flank of the Beacon, on a very clear rocky path through the heather. The Bronze Age tumulus known as Little Rowbarrow is reached first, followed by the cluster at Great Rowbarrows and then the junction with the true Exmoor Ridgeway track, which is followed as it descends gradually (with a fine view back east to the massive outline of Dunkery Beacon) to the road junction on Exford Common. Carry on westwards across the common, a blaze of purple heather in summer, passing the mound of Bendels Barrow, but at the next road bear right for about 200 yards, then turn left on to Almsworthy Common.

A stone circle is marked on the map in this vicinity, and its remains can indeed be traced, due north of Greenlands. Shirley Toulson suggests that there were once ninety stones here, in three concentric circles, but the remaining stones lurking in the heather and bilberries give no impression of grandeur on that scale. Further north-west near the track, which keeps close to a hedge, is the real reason for this slight diversion from the ridgeway – Alderman's Barrow, a fine Bronze Age bowl barrow with a shallow depression in the centre of its circular mound. Much later it attained renewed importance as one of the boundary markers of Exmoor Forest.

To regain the ridgeway, walk back south-west along the road to a sharp bend where a track strikes off westwards, but keep to the crest of the flat-topped ridge as it runs north of the headwaters of the River Exe. Navigational skills and water-repellent footwear are the main ingredients of success in traversing this inhospitable upland as far as Blackpits Gate, some 3 miles away over the level and largely featureless moor. Matters take some time to improve from here, too, although a track can be picked up across Exe Plain and past a woebegone tumulus to the greater eminence of Chains Barrow, topped by an OS pillar and widely known for its excellent view of the heart of Exmoor.

Chains Barrow lies just to the north of the South Chains Wall, part of the forest wall constructed in the 1820s by John Knight as part of his improvements. Significantly, he did not include the Chains within his wall, for even he had to accept that it was incapable of cultivation – and rightly so, for this area of deer-sedge bog lying at around 1,500ft is plagued by acidic soils and a water table trapped near ground level by an impenetrable 'iron pan'. It is imperative to return to the South Chains Wall and its accompanying path to make further progress west along the ridge.

The South Chains Wall does in fact lead directly to the dam impounding Pinkworthy Pond – the source of the River Barle and another of John Knight's schemes. He employed Irish labourers to drown this 7 acre hollow in the brooding emptiness of the Chains. Burton describes it as 'the enigma of the moor', for even Knight's papers fail to make clear the purpose of the pond. A short length of abandoned canal south of Pinkworthy is equally mysterious, since it has no link to the pond and even if one had been intended Pinkworthy could not have provided sufficient water to fill it. The pond has seen its share of tragedy and is reputedly haunted by a farmer who drowned himself in its depths in 1880.

Not far away from Pinkworthy Pond, again via the South Chains Wall, is Wood Barrow, another round barrow which has been used to mark both the forest boundary and the county boundary between Somerset and Devon. Further west are still more tumuli, one of them designated the Longstone Barrow because of its proximity to the Longstone, unattractively located in a slight depression which is usually wet underfoot but nevertheless a powerful monument to its Bronze Age creators. Exactly why this crooked, 9ft high slaty monolith, the best of Exmoor's standing stones, was erected here is something of a mystery since it is not all that conspicuous except from the minor valley of Swincombe. Perhaps, in one of those failures of communication which still bedevil the construction industry, it was simply erected in the wrong place.

The next slight rise in the ridge is the location of Chapman Barrows (SS690434), a highly evocative group of eleven (some say twelve) burial mounds on the ridge line above Challacombe Common. This cluster of tumuli forms one of the great Bronze Age monuments of Exmoor. The great bowl-shaped barrows, about 100ft in diameter and up to 12ft high, lie in a superb setting close to the line of the ridgeway almost 1,600ft above sea-level, with an outlook northwards to the Bristol Channel, east over Exmoor Forest and southwards towards Dartmoor. One of the barrows was opened in 1885 by a farm labourer, who found bones in an urn located in a stone chamber right at the centre.

The ridge continues westwards towards the depressing main-road hamlet of Blackmoor Gate, but there is no obvious path and the way off the moor is difficult. Of the two other routes, the way down to Challacombe, on a clear track past the abandoned Domesday manor of Radworthy and the farm at Withycombe is pleasant enough, but I would recommend descending close to Highley and Holwell Castle to finish the walk at Parracombe (itself noted for the memorable interior of St Petrock's church, with its Georgian box pews and other furnishings).

Notes

Maps   OS 1:50,000 sheets 180 and 181.
Further reading   S. H. Burton, *Exmoor* (Robert Hale, 1974); Countryside Commission, *Exmoor National Park Guide* (HMSO, 1970); Shirley Toulson, *The Moors of the Southwest: Exploring the Ancient Tracks of Sedgemoor and Exmoor* (Hutchinson, 1983).
Public transport   Wheddon Cross has a notably poor bus service: one morning bus from Minehead each weekday, and another at lunchtime (except Thursdays). The Dulverton community bus also provides a single service on Fridays. There are four buses a day from Lynton to Barnstaple, passing through Parracombe and Blackmoor Gate.

12

THE ROMAN ROAD
FROM NEATH TO BRECON

Coelbren to Brecon 18 miles/29km

Although this was a minor link road in Roman times and it has in some places subsequently fallen into disuse, this route has the distinction of passing through the impressive scenery of the Brecon Beacons, with easy route-finding along green tracks in the foothills of the high mountains. Amongst the attractions are the standing stones of Maen Madoc and Maen Llia, and the trek across Mynydd Illtyd Common, with the superb northern scarp face of the Beacons prominently in view.

Historical Background

Roman power in South Wales was organised around two east–west and two north–south roads: westwards from Hereford to Llandovery, and from Caerleon to Carmarthen, and northwards from Carmarthen to north-west Wales and from Caerleon through the Welsh Marches to Chester. Within this framework less important roads were built to link forts on the principal routes, and the road from Neath to Brecon did just that, connecting Y Gaer (3 miles west of Brecon) with Nidum (Neath). In so doing it ploughed through the Brecon Beacons, reaching a height of 1,400ft on the southern shoulder of Fan Nedd.

It is generally accepted that the Romans policed Wales instead of trying to tame the natives and cultivate the countryside, and so it is hardly surprising to find that Y Gaer, constructed about 75 AD and occupied initially by a garrison of 500 Spanish cavalrymen, was abandoned as early as 200 AD. The Roman road, which later became known (like so many others in Wales) as Sarn Helen after the fourth-century wife of Emperor Magnus Maximus, was probably never heavily used and was left to decay after the Romans departed.

This neglect continued unabated through the medieval period, aided by the fact that most of the route lay within Fforest Fawr, the Great Forest – 50 square miles of mountains maintained as a massive deer park until its enclosure and conversion to sheep pasture in the nineteenth century. Enclosure coincided with the heyday of the droving trade, and parts of the

74

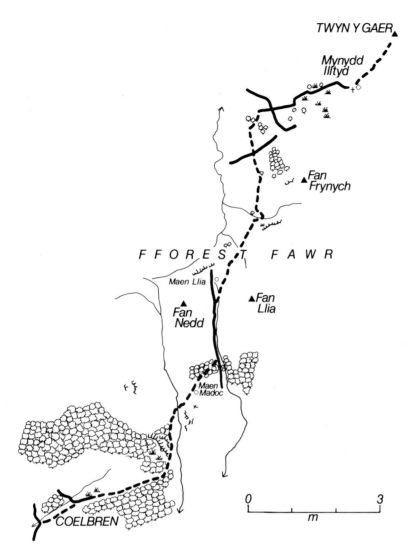

ancient route were pressed into service as a section of the drove road to Brecon and the English markets, before subsiding once again into the quiet green lanes which now characterise much of the course of the Roman road.

Description of the Route

This walk across the Brecon Beacons National Park ironically starts in much less attractive surroundings just outside the park boundary at the Roman fort near Coelbren (SN858107). To the south and east is the massive opencast coal site around Onllwyn and Banwen Pyrddin. The fort itself, though it can easily be made out in the marshes of Gors Llwyn, consists of little more than a gently rounded swelling in the grassy plateau.

75

Sarn Helen left Coelbren fort to the north-east, but for the first ½ mile or so there is no right of way (though the Roman agger is very striking here and this section is in fact scheduled as an Ancient Monument), and a diversion is necessary – either south-east along the farm lane to Dysgwylfa and then northwards to Cefngwaunhynog, or north-west towards Coelbren and then east along a lane to Cefngwaunhynog. The second route is better, not least because it allows an extra but very short detour to Sgwd Henrhyd – a spectacular waterfall where the Nant Llech falls about 90ft over a cliff where a thin seam of coal has been exposed.

To the east of Cefngwaunhynog the lane, which is now on the Roman alignment, soon peters out into a green track running along the northern edge of the Forestry Commission plantation known as Coed y Rhaiadr (Waterfall Wood), with rather damp rough pasture to the left of the track. This is a particularly remote area, with nothing but the ruins of Gors-wen Farm, buried in the forest, and a few reminders of forestry activities between Cefngwaunhynog and Blaen-nedd-isaf, some 3 miles away.

The Roman road, normally marking the forest boundary, contours the hillside above the Afon Nedd (River Neath) at about 1,100ft, maintaining its appearance as a well-defined green lane. To the north-west of Pwll-y-rhyd, where a narrow bridge has replaced the old ford (though the Nedd often flows underground at this point) there is a complicated junction of tracks. One drove-like lane is enclosed between limestone walls, but the route lies to the right of this, through a tall gate and down a graded track to cross the Afon Nedd above Blaen-nedd-isaf Farm.

The course of the Roman road above Blaen-nedd-isaf, looking towards Fan Nedd

For some time now the rounded grassy hump of Fan Nedd (2,176ft/663m) has dominated the northern view, and the Roman road has to surmount this obstacle on its way to Y Gaer. The chosen course keeps well to the south of the summit itself, climbing steadily to cross the ridge at nearly 1,400ft. Here is the standing stone of Maen Madoc, a tall and quite slender inscribed pillar reputedly dating from the early days of the Kingdom of Brycheiniog in the fifth or sixth century AD. The inscription, now illegible, was in Latin and reputedly commemorated the death and burial place of Dervacus, son of Justus, though despite excavation no trace of the burial has been found.

Now the route runs through another forestry plantation to reach the minor road linking Ystradfellte with Heol Senni. The road, which keeps to the western side of the wide, shallow upper valley of the Afon Llia, can be quite busy in summer and it may be with some relief that the track branching off to the right after about a mile is reached. This narrow track, roughly surfaced to begin with, is on the Roman route but was also much used in the eighteenth and nineteenth centuries by drovers bringing stock from West Wales to Brecon and the east. The track quickly descends to the river and crosses it at Rhyd Uchaf (the upper ford), then climbs away from the flood plain to cross the spur of Bryn Melyn as a sunken road and reach a terrace below the cliffs of Craig Cwm-du.

Shortly beyond Rhyd Uchaf a second standing stone, Maen Llia, can be seen on the left, and like Maen Madoc it repays inspection. Another Early Christian inscribed stone, it is much broader than Maen Madoc and commands a very wide view along the valley of the Afon Llia to Ystradfellte and the wooded hill slopes beyond. Various theories have been put forward to explain its position, and it has variously been described as a gravestone, route-marker and boundary stone; it may indeed have served all of these purposes.

The moorland track from Bryn Melyn is here skirting the lower reaches of Fforest Fawr, originally a royal hunting ground but now mostly rough grazing – although there are inevitable pressures to convert parts to forestry and the view of Fan Gihyrch, to the west, will change as planting takes place. The track descends slightly to cross Nant Cwm-du at Pont Blaen-cwm-du (the bridge at the head of the black valley – a reference to the forbidding scarp slopes above the track). East of Gelliau-ganol the drovers' road swings sharply right, to pass below Fan Frynych, but the Roman road appears to have kept on northwards for a while, then turned north-east (its course no longer followed by rights of way) to reach Mynydd Illtyd Common near Felincamlais.

In the circumstances the best course of action is to follow the drove road above Blaenbryich and Forest Lodge to the A4215 at Ffynnon-ynys-gron, and

The Early Christian inscribed stone of Maen Llia

then to take the track back across the Common towards Felincamlais to see an exposed section of the Roman road, its course slightly raised, just at the western edge of the Common. (The overgrown motte to the north, the remains of the thirteenth-century Blaencamlais Castle, is on private ground and cannot be visited; there are, however, glimpses of the motte, surrounded by a deep ditch, and surmounted by the ruins of a tower which once stood 50ft high.)

Keep parallel to the road across the common, but not too far south of it, skirting the treacherous bog known as Traeth Mawr. The views south are quite stupendous, with the magnificent escarpment of the Brecon Beacons dominating the skyline (Pen y Fan, 2,906ft/886m is the highest summit), and a good view also of the other mountain ranges in the National Park – the Black Mountains to the east, Fforest Fawr south and Y Mynydd Du south-west. At a road junction another section of Sarn Helen can be seen to the north, but there is no through route here and it is better to turn south to visit Llanilltyd church.

The church itself is modern, dating only from 1858, and is disused, but the large circular churchyard is thought to date from the time of St Illtyd, one of the early Christian saints. Bedd Illtyd, to the north-east, was once supposed to be the burial place of the saint, but it is now accepted as a Bronze Age tumulus. Across the common from here is the mountain centre, built specifically for the purpose in 1966 and functioning as an information centre and café. From the centre a track leads across the eastern part of the common, again with remarkable mountain views, to the OS pillar on the summit of Twyn y Gaer.

The hilltop settlement of Twyn y Gaer, defined by a single ditch and low rampart and with an eastern entrance, dates from the Iron Age and was probably inhabited only in times of war. It has a fine bird's-eye view of the Usk valley, with the fortified farm of Aber-Bran Fawr due north and Penpont House, seventeenth century with a later colonnaded front, north-west. Across the Usk is Mynydd Eppynt, a massive plateau now largely commandeered by the Army; and beyond Brecon to the east the Black Mountains are seen end-on from Hay Bluff in the north through Waun Fach and Pen-y-Gader-Fawr, the highest tops, to the southern outlier of the Sugar Loaf.

The Roman road at the eastern end of Twyn y Gaer is obviously pointing to the fort at Y Gaer, but its course towards it is lost, and so too is the point at which it crossed the River Usk. In the absence of a modern bridge there is no

The southern approach to the hill-fort on the summit of Twyn y Gaer

alternative but to walk to Brecon, with the possibility of a separate visit to Y Gaer, where the excavated remains of three gateways, angle turrets and a section of the external wall are visible behind a farmhouse.

A minor road leads directly from Twyn y Gaer to Brecon (SO043286) but the amount of road walking can be reduced to a minimum by the judicious use of footpaths. Perhaps the best of these descends eastwards from near the hill-fort to Cefn-y-Parc Farm and, via a farm road, to the main road (A40) and chapel at Llanspyddid. The River Usk runs just to the north of the A40 here, and from just east of Llanspyddid a riverside footpath is shown on the map, passing a golf course and Newton Pool into Llanfaes, effectively a suburb of the cathedral city, Norman castle town and medieval market town of Brecon.

Notes

Maps OS 1:25,000 Outdoor Leisure sheets 12 and 11 (Brecon Beacons National Park – Western and Central) or 1:50,000 sheet 160.

Further reading Ivan Margary, *Roman Roads in Britain* (John Baker, 3rd edn. 1973); Edward J. Mason, *Portrait of the Brecon Beacons* (Robert Hale, 1975).

Accommodation Don't rely on finding any in the vicinity of Coelbren; plentiful in Brecon.

Public transport There is an hourly bus service from Swansea and Neath to Banwen Pyrddin, close to Coelbren Roman fort. Brecon has nine buses a day (two on Sundays) to Abergavenny and six buses a day (again two on Sundays) to Merthyr Tydfil and Cardiff.

13

SARN HELEN (EAST)

Llandovery to Llanfair Clydogau 16 miles/26km

The route traces the Roman road from Llandovery to Caeo, the Roman gold mines at Dolaucothi, the hamlets of Pumsaint and Farmers, and finally Llanfair Clydogau, near Lampeter. An easy walk, partly on country lanes, reaching a maximum height of 1,215ft (370m), but with wide views to the Black Mountain and to Cardigan Bay.

Historical Background

Roman rule in south Wales was, as shown in the previous chapter, organised around a quadrilateral of roads whose southern base connected Caerleon and Carmarthen, with roads striking north from each of those fortresses to Chester and north-west Wales respectively. But there was also an important link road from Caerleon to Brecon and Llandovery, joining the west Wales road at Bremia, north of Lampeter. The last section of this link road has also attracted the name of Sarn Helen, and to avoid confusion it is referred to here as Sarn Helen (East).

This link road approached Llandovery from the south-east across the northern outposts of the Black Mountain, and this route was still in use as the main coach road from Brecon to Llandovery in the eighteenth century. Now it is merely a rough track across desolate moorland, with the earthworks of the fort called Y Pigwn still visible.

Llandovery, too, had a Roman fort, whose main purpose was to guard the approaches to the gold mines at Dolaucothi. For Sarn Helen was not just a link road: it led to gold mines which had been worked in prehistoric times and were finally abandoned as recently as 1938. A small fort, located where the hamlet of Pumsaint now stands, provided on-the-spot protection for the miners.

The route of Sarn Helen (East) has been traced in its entirety, although one or two small sections have fallen into disuse. From Llandovery it climbs Heol Rhos to Porthyrhyd, becomes a track descending a holloway to Aberbowlan, and reaches Dolaucothi and Pumsaint. Beyond Pumsaint the Roman road changes course to a more northerly alignment to reach Sarn Helen proper at Llanfair Clydogau.

81

Caeo from the south-west

After the departure of the Romans the road may have been abandoned as a through route, though parts were still used and the gold mines appear to have continued in production. Traffic increased greatly, however, with the coming of the drovers. Cattle were certainly being driven from Wales to southern England in the fourteenth century, and the Act of Union greatly increased this trade. By the sixteenth century the drove roads led across upland Wales and along the 'Welsh roads' through England to markets as far distant as Northampton, Barnet and Maidstone.

Description of the Route

Before leaving Llandovery (SN767343) it is worth having a look around the little market town. The grassy banks of the Roman fort lie ½ mile to the north-east of the centre, and the church of St Mary, built inside the fort, has some long, narrow Roman bricks in its east wall. To the south of the town the medieval castle stands between the river and the cattle market. The town hall and market hall lie immediately across the main road, whilst along the street

Lloyds Bank was formerly the Black Ox Bank, established in 1799 by the drover David Jones and one of the earliest banks in Wales.

Take the A40 out of Llandovery towards Llandeilo, cross the Afon Tywi, ignore the turning on the right to Cilycwm and Rhandirmwyn, and take the unmarked lane known as Heol Rhos a further hundred yards on the right. This lane, which follows the alignment of Sarn Helen (East), climbs steadily for a while, then crosses a small valley. East of Cnwcdeilog the road curves gently left and then right, but the straight line of the Roman road is

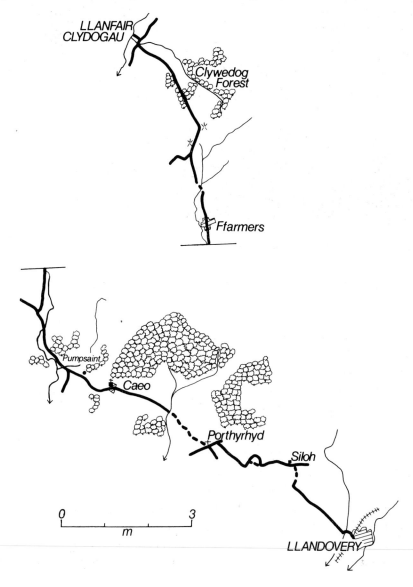

perpetuated by a series of hedgerows – an alignment which is especially obvious from above, where the present lane rejoins the Romans' route.

Turn right at a crossroads and after passing a wayside chapel turn left into Siloh, a moorland hamlet where New Inn Farm is the successor to a drovers' pub. At Ysgrafell a track cuts off a wide detour around a wooded ravine. As height is gained the views become increasingly spectacular, with the Carmarthen Fan and the Black Mountain silhouetted on the southern skyline. After ½ mile follow the road round to the left into the hamlet of Porthyrhyd, where Drovers Farm is another reminder of former times.

Beyond a chapel a track leads steeply up to the right, past Banc Bedwgleision (literally 'the bank of the blue birches') to Aberbowlan. This is one of the highlights of the walk, with firm turf underfoot and excellent views of Caeo Forest to the north and west. From the highest point, a mere 948ft (289m), the way lies down a splendid rutted holloway, with a typically Roman zigzag in the steepest section, to a ford over the Afon Dulais and then up a short lane to the former droving stance of Aberbowlan, nestling amongst its Scots pines.

Turn right along the road, then curve left around the farm buildings and head towards Caeo. Beyond Albert Mount there is a sudden 'aerial' view of the village of Caeo, dominated by the huge grey tower of its church. Embedded in the north wall of the church is a Latin-inscribed monolith, and indeed Caeo was described by an early Welsh poet as a town built of thin red Roman bricks. Once famous as a cattle-dealing centre and collecting point for the English droves, Caeo is now just a quiet backwater.

Cross the Afon Annell and immediately turn right, to climb very steeply up a narrow lane making for Pumsaint. Half-way along this lane look down to the right into the hummocky area containing the Roman and later gold mines at Dolaucothi. The only place in Britain where the Romans are definitely known to have mined gold, Dolaucothi has been described as the most technically advanced Roman industrial site in the country.

Although the mines were worked sporadically before the Romans arrived, their superior organisation and technical ability enabled real exploitation to begin. Water-power was used, and an elaborate series of aqueducts was constructed; the Cothi aqueduct, 7 miles long, was cut into the hillside, sometimes through solid rock, and could provide some 3 million gallons of water a day. The aqueduct can be seen as a stone-lined ditch entering a former reservoir just above the mines.

The gold mines appear to have been worked in medieval times, and as late as the 1930s 200 people were employed, but the venture proved uneconomic and mining finally ended in 1938. The gold mines and the surrounding area are now owned by the National Trust, and there are a number of excellent

The entrance to one of the gold mines at Dolaucothi

short walks in and around the workings. A visitor centre has recently been opened, and guided tours of the underground workings are available between July and September.

Near the National Trust car park is an open space dominated by Carreg Pumsaint, a rock pillar with indentations on all sides. These hollows are said to have been made by the shoulders of five saints – Gwyn, Gwyno, Gwynoro, Celynin and Ceitho – who spent a stormy night huddled against the rock. Whatever the truth of the story, the five saints have inspired the name of the village of Pumsaint, which is reached by taking the road leading west from the mines to the main road and then crossing the Afon Cothi.

There are no visible remains of the Roman fort of Pumsaint, although excavation has proved that it underlies the modern village. It covered about 5 acres, included a stone granary together with workshops and a barrack block, and was probably abandoned by about the end of the second century, by which time all Welsh resistance had been crushed. Further south, on the banks of the Cothi, there was a small bath-house.

George Borrow stayed at the 'inn of the Pump Saint' and observed that 'the village consists of little more than half a dozen houses'. There are more than that now, scattered thinly along the main road, which coincides with Sarn Helen (East) for a little over a mile, as far as the bridge over the Afon Twrch. The blacksmith's shop which Borrow noticed is now a garage, but the toll-house which the drovers knew still stands.

Just beyond the Afon Twrch take the very narrow lane to the right, then turn right along the road to the village of Farmers. This is the point at which Sarn Helen (East) changes course to the north, heading up the valley of the Afon Twrch to Farmers, which took its name from the Farmers Inn, now the post office; the Drovers Arms, immediately opposite, is still licensed. Droves were assembled and deals struck in the road between the two, and the

Carreg Pumsaint

blacksmith was based in the field north of the Farmers Inn.

Sarn Helen (East) now heads for lonelier country at the head of the Twrch, turning left down a steep and narrow lane and crossing the Twrch for the last time by means of a wide ford with a footbridge alongside. This twisting lane, with the derelict embankments of the Roman road in the fields to its left, climbs to join the mountain road crossing the Craig Twrch ridge, with its rocky turrets, at a low col. There are superb retrospective views over the Twrch valley and the Cothi woods to the Black Mountain, and in front, as the highest ground is reached, there are equally fine views over the Teifi valley to the Cardigan Bay coastline, and over the bleak, forested tracts of the Cambrian mountain foothills.

As Sarn Helen (East) loses height it straightens and heads north-west through Forestry Commission woodland – part of Aeron Forest. Buried in the forest is the site of what the 6in OS map describes as 'Roman practice work'. It is possible to find the site, in an unplanted oblong a hundred yards into the forest, but the effort is scarcely worth while. There are a few mounds and trenches in the long grass, but they can surely represent little more than the efforts of a few apprentices let loose on a spare afternoon. More tangible are the roofless remains of a few abandoned cottages, eerily dotted about amongst the trees.

The Roman road (this section of which later formed part of yet another drove road) loses height gradually and uneventfully, and finally reaches the B4343 and Sarn Helen proper on the outskirts of Llanfair Clydogau (SN624512). The west-coast Roman road ran north from here to Conwy, and south to Lampeter (3 miles away by minor road or bridlepath) and Carmarthen. But the scattered village of Llanfair Clydogau marks the end of Sarn Helen (East) and of this walk.

Notes

Map   OS 1:50,000 sheet 146.
Further reading   George Borrow, *Wild Wales* (Collins, 1862); Fay Godwin and Shirley Toulson, *The Drovers' Roads of Wales* (Wildwood House, 1977); Ivan Margary, *Roman Roads in Britain* (John Baker, 3rd edn. 1973); Joanna Methuen-Campbell, *The Roman Gold Mines at Dolaucothi* (National Trust, n.d.)
Public transport   Llandovery is on the Central Wales railway line (five trains in each direction on weekdays) and there are also buses to Brecon, Cheltenham and Swansea. Lampeter has an express bus service to Swansea (this service also calls at Pumsaint) and buses to Carmarthen and Aberystwyth.

14

THE KERRY HILLS RIDGEWAY

Cider House to Bishop's Castle 14 miles/22km

An excellent and very varied walk in the remote hills of the Welsh Borders, following a prehistoric trackway which later formed part of a very important drovers' route. The walk traverses the ridge of Kerry Hill itself, then passes through forestry plantations where the track forms the border between England and Wales for several miles, crosses a particularly impressive stretch of Offa's Dyke and ends in the very quiet market town of Bishop's Castle.

Historical Background

A number of important prehistoric through routes appear to have traversed the hills around the headwaters of the Teme and Clun. Chief among these was the Clun-Clee ridgeway, which has been traced from Kerry Pole past Bettws-y-Crwyn, Spoad Hill and Clungunford to Titterstone Clee Hill. The Kerry Hills ridgeway kept to a more northerly course from Kerry Pole, passing through Bishopsmoat and Bishop's Castle. Even further north a prehistoric trackway known as Yr Hen Ffordd (the Old Road) crosses Stapeley Hill. Travellers on the second and third of these routes could have then continued across the Long Mynd using the Portway, another apparently pre-Roman trackway.

The Kerry Hills ridgeway, often described as the oldest road in Wales, appears to have come into use in the early Bronze Age – perhaps as early as 2000 BC. Its importance lay in its use by traders carrying roughly hewn axe-heads eastwards (from the picrite outcrop on the slopes of Corndon Hill, close to the route), and flint implements westwards. The flints must have originated in a chalk outcrop, the nearest of which is over 100 miles away, in the Marlborough Downs. It is even possible that the track was used by Irish traders as an alternative to the more northerly coastal route, and it is still infrequently referred to as 'the Irish ridgeway'.

In the later Bronze Age the significance of the trackway appears to have declined, mainly because of climatic changes which encouraged the formation of peat bogs over the uplands. For many centuries the ridgeway was relegated to minor-route status, though its existence was never forgotten:

Bishops Castle

when Offa's Dyke was constructed in the eighth century it was especially well fortified in the vicinity of the ridgeway, and it appears that three outlying earthworks – the Cross Dyke, Upper Short Ditch and Lower Short Ditch – were constructed further west at the same time to give added security. Later it became the county boundary between Shropshire and Montgomery – and hence eventually the national boundary between England and Wales.

The Kerry Hills trackway regained its former prominence in the later medieval period, when it became one of the great Welsh drove roads. Although droving had become a staple Welsh industry by the thirteenth century, and was so important that the cattle farmers of North Wales petitioned the King during the Civil War, pleading with him to keep the droveways to Shrewsbury open, the trade reached its peak much later and remained crucial until the tentacles of the railway spread as far as the border market towns in the 1850s.

Two almost parallel drove routes ran through the central border hills: one made for the great collecting centre of Montgomery and then led south-eastwards to Plowden, at the foot of the Long Mynd, while the other used the ancient Kerry Hills track to Bishop's Castle before turning north-east. The twin streams of cattle converged at Plowden, crossed the Long Mynd via the Portway, and gained the valley road to Shrewsbury at Leebotwood, where the name of the Pound Inn still reflects the importance of the droving trade.

Description of the Route

Sadly the Cider House (SO108846), starting-point of the walk, is a shadow of its former self, selling no cider and now consisting of a farm complex patched up with rusty corrugated iron. On the opposite side of the B4355 the ridge track begins, though there is no signpost. Go through the gate and keep to the track as it rises steadily towards the summit plateau of the whale-backed Kerry Hill. Gradually the view becomes more all-embracing, especially to the north, over the Mule valley towards Newtown, and westwards past the Cider House and its adjoining woodland to the hills above Llanidloes.

After half a mile the track passes through a gate and then breaches the Cross Dyke, a remarkably well-preserved delaying tactic which simply aimed to disrupt traffic using the border way in times of strife. The dyke is still 4–5ft deep and together with its accompanying banks once blocked the entire ridge top (the lowlands on either side were so thickly wooded as to be impassable). Just beyond the Cross Dyke the track reaches its highest point, 1,657ft, and passes the Two Tumps, round barrows which later served as an easily recognisable collecting point for the cattle drovers.

The ridge top is flat and, as the result of the accumulation of peat,

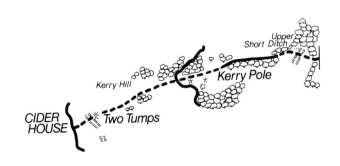

excessively boggy in places, although the worst patches can usually be skirted close to the fence. Unfriendly notices warning of bulls in the fields crossed by the public bridleway might not induce confidence, but though they should not be dismissed lightly the risk of confrontation is small. The trackway runs almost dead straight along the ridge, past Radnorshire Gate, across the B4368, through Black Wood and down to the little cluster of buildings at Kerry Pole. Just before this a path to the right leads past a tumulus to the scanty remains of a stone circle.

At Kerry Pole roads lead both to the left, to the village of Kerry (where in 1176 the Bishop of St Asaph and Archdeacon of Brecon excommunicated each other on the spot in a dispute over diocesan boundaries) and to the right, along the line of the Clun-Clee ridgeway to Anchor Inn, Bettws-y-Crwyn and Clun. But the Kerry Hills ridgeway keeps to the high ground as a narrow lane passing another burial mound and becoming increasingly hemmed in by forestry plantations. Some way to the east of Cefngolog a second blocking exercise of the Saxon era, the Upper Short Ditch, had to be negotiated by earlier travellers; now it is only a minor indentation on the landscape. Even odder, ½ mile further east, is the Cantlin Stone, a modern replacement of an older monument to a pedlar who was found robbed and murdered here in 1691. After an unseemly delay he was finally buried in the churchyard at Bettws-y-Crwyn, 4 miles away.

The trackway is now passing through the Long Plantation, part of Clun Forest, and since Cefngolog it has formed the national boundary. Towards the end of the forest yet another cross-dyke formerly had to be negotiated. This is the Lower Short Ditch, still quite impressive in places along its course between Hopton Bank and Ditch Dingle. Yet another plantation looms on the right: this is the Turbury Plantation, its name possibly a reference to peat-cutting (as on the slopes of Gragareth and Whernside, noted in the Craven Way chapter).

The ridgeway, now a roughly surfaced narrow lane, drops steeply down the spur separating the River Unk (soon to turn south and pass through Mainstone, a quiet village which was once quite an important market centre)

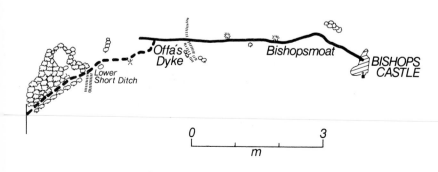

The massive bank and ditch (the latter now occupied by a sunken lane) of Offa's Dyke to the west of Hazel Bank

from tributaries of the Camlad, and arrives at the extensive and in parts dilapidated complex of farm buildings at Pantglas. Here a minor road, generally used only by local farm traffic, leads east towards Bishop's Castle, again keeping to the higher ground. After half a mile the magnificent earthwork of Offa's Dyke intersects the route. To the left, it accompanies a sunken lane leading down to Crowsnest Cottage, and the 10ft high bank is particularly impressive. To the right, after a short footpath through trees, the ditch and massive bank are even more conspicuous, running to the east of Nut Wood and with wide views to the border hills.

The country lane maintains a notably straight course past Hazel Bank, where Dog and Duck Cottage hints at a former use, and the gorse-ridden minor earthwork at Caer Din, which is of uncertain date and may even have been a Roman outpost. There are good views north-east of Corndon Hill and the start of the Long Mynd on the way down to the cluster of houses at Bishopsmoat. The moat itself, actually the remains of a motte-and-bailey

The tower brewery in the yard of the Three Tuns, Bishops Castle

castle, constructed as a defence against Welsh incursions from the upper Severn valley, comes as something of a surprise, with a fine circular motte which is bigger than one might expect in such an isolated spot and a well-preserved pattern of ditches defining the adjacent bailey.

Now the way lies along the declining ridge of Moat Hill, keeping straight on when the road forks. The boundary between England and Wales at last departs to the north as the lane runs through Bankshead, with a widening prospect south-eastwards to the well-wooded hills around Bury Ditches hill-fort. Finally the diminutive market town of Bishop's Castle is entered, appropriately along Welsh Street. The twelfth-century new town took its name from another motte-and-bailey castle; this is well hidden behind the Castle Hotel, but there is still plenty to see.

The Market Square (SO323890), small though it is, is a reminder of the former status of the town, which used to send two Members of Parliament to Westminster and was a municipal borough until 1965. The brick town hall is either imposing or appalling according to taste; to one side is the picturesque House on Crutches, its upper storey supported on timber posts. On Salop Street is the Three Tuns, with a history dating back to 1642 and a working brewery attached to the pub. The main street drops steeply down from the town hall to the church, its sturdy Norman tower a reminder of its defensive role in post-Conquest times. Nowadays the town is in decline and looks a little down at heel; tourism may arrive too late to save it.

Notes

Maps   OS 1:50,000 sheets 136 and 137.

Further reading   Fay Godwin and Shirley Toulson, *The Drovers' Roads of Wales* (Wildwood House, 1977); Roy Millward and Adrian Robinson, *The Welsh Borders* (Eyre Methuen, 1978); Trevor Rowley, *The Shropshire Landscape* (Hodder & Stoughton, 1972).

Public transport   There are no public transport services in the vicinity of the Cider House, but Newtown station (only 4 miles away) is on the Shrewsbury to Machynlleth railway line. Bishop's Castle has a regular bus service to Shrewsbury (Minsterley Motors, approximately two-hourly) and also a Friday afternoon bus to Ludlow.

15

THE OLD PENRHYN ROAD

Capel Curig to Bethesda 9 miles/14km

Constructed in 1791 to link Lord Penrhyn's lands at Capel Curig and Bethesda, the Old Road had a remarkably short life-span as a main route: it was succeeded in 1805 by a turnpike road on the opposite side of the valley, and this road was itself superseded by Telford's markedly superior road, the forerunner of the present A5, in 1826. But the Old Road can be followed throughout its length and provides an excellent, easy walk with stupendous views of the craggy mountains at the heart of Snowdonia.

Historical Background

The notion that the Old Road had Roman origins is still perpetuated in some books, but in fact it is one of the newest roads included in this book, dating back only to 1791 as a through route (though small parts of it in the Nant Ffrancon valley may have been in local use previously). It is 'old' only in comparison with its successors on the far side of the Ogwen and Llugwy valleys.

Ogwen Cottage

The major difficulty confronting road-makers in the Ogwen valley was the 200ft high rock step at the western end of Llyn Ogwen, where the river cascades over the Ogwen Falls into the flat, heavily glaciated trough of Nant Ffrancon. Lord Penrhyn, however, had not only the determination but also the money to surmount this difficulty and create a through route, since he owned the vastly profitable slate quarries which still disfigure the side of Carnedd y Filiast above Bethesda.

Much of the quarry land was illegally enclosed (and thereby stolen from its owners, the Crown), the quarry workers were ill-paid, and Penrhyn's attitude to trade unions and strikes was heavy-handed and authoritarian: yet amongst the outcomes of his Lordship's endeavours were a model village for the workers at Llandegai and the Old Road, at last opening up the heart of Snowdonia to wheeled traffic. Lord Penrhyn's intentions were not philanthropic, though: he owned an estate at Capel Curig and even at this early stage was able to see its tourist potential. He built an hotel at Capel Curig – the former Royal Hotel, now the Plas y Brenin outdoor pursuits centre – and began to cater for the embryonic taste for mountain exploration.

Penrhyn's road left Bethesda on what is now the A5, but soon crossed the Afon Ogwen and followed the western side of the Nant Ffrancon valley, keeping just above the Ogwen flood plain. South of Blaen-y-Nant it climbed steadily towards Pont Pen-y-Benglog (where an early packhorse track had been described in 1773 as 'the most dreadful horse-path in Wales') and Llyn Ogwen, crossed the watershed into the Llugwy valley and kept south of the river until crossing it on a high stone bridge to enter Capel Curig.

The Old Road quickly proved incapable of handling the traffic, however, and increasing demands for a high-class inland route to Holyhead led to the construction of a turnpike road in 1805, on the northern and eastern valley slopes. Yet even this new road quickly fell into disrepair, becoming worn and deeply rutted where the foundations were inadequate. The mail coach service was withdrawn, to the dismay of Irish Members of Parliament, whose protests led to the establishment of a Parliamentary Commission, advised by Thomas Telford. Telford's improved turnpike road, completed in 1826, now forms the route of the A5.

Description of the Route

The old Penrhyn road leaves the huddle of shops and cottages at the heart of Capel Curig within a few yards of the triangle formed by the junction of the A5 with the A4086 to Beddgelert (SH721581). Take the lane leading past Joe Brown's mountain shop, negotiate a steep ladder-stile and cross the Hen Bont (Old Bridge) over the Afon Llugwy. Unremarkable from above, the

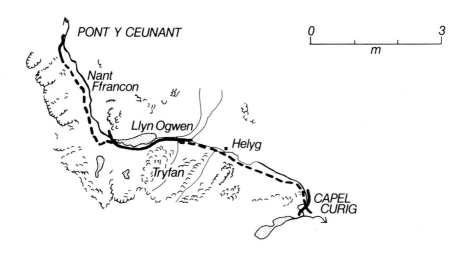

bridge assumes a greater status when seen from either side, for now it is revealed as disproportionately tall and massive – eloquent testimony to the raging torrent into which the normally placid Afon Llugwy can be transformed after prolonged heavy rain.

For the length of a field the Old Road is a narrow tarmac lane serving Gelli cottage, seen ahead and to the left. Already there is a fine view away to the south-west, across Llynnau Mymbyr towards the Snowdon massif. Go through the gate at the end of the field, pass a ruined cottage and swing round below Creigiau'r Gelli, with the Old Road now a grassy track and only the sound of traffic on the A5, across the Llugwy valley, dispelling the feeling of solitude.

After an initial climb the Old Road maintains a fairly level and sometimes slightly damp course to the south of the river. On the left are the beginnings of the Glyder range, although initially the magnificent prospect of the high ground in front is obscured by the projecting spur of Gallt yr Ogof. Later, however, as the isolated climbing hut of Helyg (described by George Borrow in 1862 as 'a wretched hovel') is approached the first memorable sight of the eastern ramparts of Tryfan is gained. The whole of the east face is a mass of bare rock, plunging precipitously down from a jagged skyline, at the apex of which are the twin columnar rocks known as Adam and Eve.

At a much lower altitude Lord Penrhyn's road continues past Gwern Gof Isaf Farm, still as a grassy track across the Llugwy valley from the A5, then tackles the indeterminate watershed between the Llugwy and Ogwen valleys and, west of Gwern Gof Uchaf and beneath the towering cliffs of Tryfan, converges with the main road close to the head of Llyn Ogwen.

The narrow valley floor between Pen-yr-Ole-Wen ('the hill of the white light') to the north and Tryfan and the Glyders to the south is almost wholly occupied by Llyn Ogwen, and the combination of mountain and lake scenery

97

is strikingly beautiful. It does, however, limit the options for roadbuilders, and so the Old Road and Telford's road, now the A5, coincide for about a mile or so to Ogwen Cottage. (The rough lower slopes of Pen-yr-Ole-Wen do carry a path around the northern shores of Llyn Ogwen, but it is hard going in places.)

Between Ogwen Cottage and the youth hostel a path, recently comprehensively repaired, leads up into Cwm Idwal, and a short detour here is strongly recommended. The cwm is a national nature reserve, of great geological and botanical interest, but its greatest glory is the superb mountain scenery, with Llyn Idwal ringed by dramatic cliffs below Y Garn, Glyder Fawr and Y Gribin, and the black chasm of Twll Du in the centre of the Devil's Kitchen.

At Ogwen Cottage there is a further dramatic development in the scenery, and the Old Road parts company with the A5 as the two roads attempt to deal with it. The drama comes in the form of the Ogwen Falls, where the outflow from Llyn Ogwen cascades over a 200ft rock step into the heavily glaciated valley of Nant Ffrancon. Telford's road bridged the Afon Ogwen here, at Pont Pen-y-Benglog, and hugged the north-eastern side of the valley, using embankments and rock cuttings as it slowly lost height. The Old Road kept to the south-western slopes, below Y Garn and Mynydd Perfedd.

To follow the Old Road take the lane forking left just west of Ogwen Cottage (now an outdoor centre, but formerly an inn) and pass between the youth hostel and a thinly wooded enclosure. Cross a cattle grid, then go right, on to a thin path threading its way between rocky outcrops. There are twin objectives here: the best views down the length of Nant Ffrancon, with its series of hanging valleys poised above the main glacial trough, and close-up views of the Ogwen Falls and Pont Pen-y-Benglog.

The descent on the Old Road is comparatively gentle as far as Blaen-y-Nant Farm, from where there is a spectacular view back to the Ogwen Falls and the rock step defining the end of Nant Ffrancon, but there is then a steeper hill down to Pentre. The Old Road keeps above the flat valley floor, however, largely to avoid the risk of flooding, and contours at about 700ft, providing a very easy walk along a narrow lane to Maes Caradoc and Tai-newyddion.

Now, below the slopes of Carnedd y Filiast ('cairn of the greyhound') and the last of Nant Ffrancon's hanging valleys, Lord Penrhyn's road finally forsakes its bench on the valley side and crosses the Afon Ogwen at Pont y Ceunant. The centre of Bethesda is still 1½ miles distant along the busy A5, but there is a useful alternative which avoids most of the road walking.

This alternative turns left (north) just before the bridge at Pont y Ceunant, skirts a wood and crosses pleasantly undulating countryside to Dolawen. Now there is no alternative to crossing the Afon Ogwen and walking along the A5, but only for about ¼ mile. Turn right just before the toll-house at

The Ogwen Falls and Pont Pen-y-Benglog

The heavily glaciated valley of Nant Ffrancon; the Old Road runs along the base of the mountains to the left

Ogwen Bank and follow an obvious path across wooded slopes opposite the awesome but scarcely attractive Penrhyn slate quarry. After ½ mile join a minor road, cross the Afon Caseg, and immediately turn left, passing Ysgol Abercaseg, to reach the main road in Bethesda (SH625664), a grey early-nineteenth-century slate-quarrying town named after its first Nonconformist chapel.

Notes

Maps   OS 1:25,000 Outdoor Leisure sheets 16 (Conwy Valley) and 17 (Snowdon) or 1:50,000 sheet 115.
Further reading   Frank Duerden, *Great Walks of North Wales* (Ward Lock, 1982); Roy Millward and Adrian Robinson, *Landscapes of North Wales* (David & Charles, 1978); Showell Styles, *The Mountains of North Wales* (Gollancz, 1973).
Public transport   From late May to late September two buses a day connect Capel Curig with Betws-y-Coed (railway station), with six buses a day at the height of the season. Three 'Snowdon Sherpa' buses a day travel between Capel Curig and Bethesda via Ogwen Cottage between late July and early September. Bethesda has frequent buses to Bangor.

16

WATLING STREET (WEST)

Church Stretton to Leintwardine 12 miles/19km

Conceived as a defensive route on the borders of the Roman Empire, Watling Street (West) connected the legionary fortresses of Deva (Chester) and Isca (Caerleon), using native trackways where these could be straightened and improved but generally breaking new ground through the Welsh Marches. The easiest section to walk today, a comfortable and surprisingly scenic walk, lies in south Shropshire and north Herefordshire.

Historical Background

The Roman advance after the invasion was so swift that the Fosse Way did not fulfil its intended function as a frontier road for long. Instead, as the Roman troops pressed on westwards a second frontier zone came into existence immediately to the east of the border hills. At an early date a road was built linking Chester and Caerleon, the crucially important legionary fortresses which controlled movement into and out of the coastal plains of North and South Wales respectively. The road, known in places as Watling Street, is referred to here as Watling Street (West) to distinguish it from the road north-west from London, much of which now forms the A5.

The road passed through Uriconium (Wroxeter), where there are substantial remains, then crossed the River Severn on a bridge which has long since ceased to exist, and ran south-west to Bravonium (Leintwardine). Main roads then mark much of its course to Magnis (Kenchester, near Hereford), and after crossing the Wye here it made for Isca (Caerleon). Ideally the walk described below would connect Wroxeter and Leintwardine, but the lack of a river-crossing at Wroxeter rules that out.

The significance of the Roman superimposition of Watling Street (West) on to the existing network of routes was that it altered an essentially east–west system of communications, dominated by the ridgeways emanating from the hills of Mid Wales, into one where the north–south route was predominant. This pattern survived the end of Roman rule, for placenames such as Stretton – which occurs three times east of the Long Mynd – and Street Court indicate that the road was still used by the Saxons. Later still the road was used to demarcate parish boundaries, another sign of its continuing importance.

Description of the Route

The first part of the route is hardest to describe, not because it is in doubt but because the 'authentic' route follows the excessively busy A49 and a search for alternatives is necessary. One possibility is to take the bus to Marshbrook, about 2½ miles away, where the main road finally parts company with its Roman counterpart. Otherwise there are three schemes worthy of consideration: the direct way along the street called Watling Street South and then the A49; the rather quieter route along the B4370 through Little Stretton; and a devious footpath route across Ragleth Hill to Ragdon, Swiss Cottage and Marshbrook.

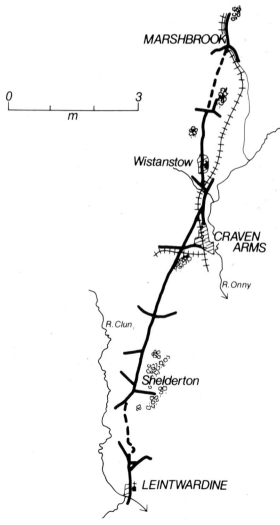

Church Stretton, that prim, staid base for the upland plateau of the Long Mynd, is worth a quick look before departing. Expanded from a mere village to a health resort in the late Victorian period, its main virtue is its situation between the Long Mynd (especially the deep combes such as the Cardingmill valley) and Caer Caradoc Hill, topped by a fine hill-fort. Little Stretton is pleasanter, boasting an unusual thatched church dating from 1903 and a number of substantial black-and-white houses.

Having arrived by one of the three routes mentioned above at Marshbrook, take the Horderley road for a few yards, passing under the railway line, then turn left along the former station approach road and quickly right on to a path skirting the right-hand edge of a copse and then skirting fields. Look back north to see the Long Mynd and Ragleth Hill, separated by the narrow gap containing the main road, its Roman predecessor and the railway. The course of the Roman road is easily followed southwards as a pleasant green lane along the field edges and through a series of gates to a junction of paths south-east of Whittingslow. From the map the obvious course seems to take the direct route to The Corner, but the Roman road apparently went through Bushmoor.

A country lane now bears the Roman route through Leamoor Common (the Roman fortlet at Woolston, ½ mile away, is described as a 'police post' by Stanford) and then Wistanstow. The village, with its Saxon church, clearly grew up along the Roman road, which may have been in continuous use for nearly 2,000 years. Wystan was a Saxon saint who was martyred in 849 AD, and the church may have been founded very soon thereafter; much of the present structure has a Norman flavour to it.

The straight road south from Wistanstow leads to the A489, then the A49 and, after ¼ mile, a lane on the line of Watling Street (West) leading past a burial mound back to the railway. A possible detour avoiding the A49 makes instead for Cheney Longville, which has a neglected but fascinating castle and may once have aspired to the status of a town – though by the middle of the twelfth century it was said to be 'so impoverished that even a stranger would not have given £15 for it'.

The course of Watling Street (West) neatly by-passes Craven Arms, but there is more than meets the eye in this superficially dull nineteenth-century railway town. The settlement actually has a much longer history, Newton (south-east of the present centre) having been a post-medieval hamlet in Stokesay parish. The location – where the B4368 'sheep road' from central Wales emerged into the Onny valley and crossed the A49 – was ideal for a market town, and by 1800 a market had been set up and the Craven Arms Inn built. But the real impetus to growth was the coming of the railway in the 1840s; after Craven Arms was chosen as a railway junction the open fields of

103

Newton were transformed into Victorian terraces (hence the gently curving form of Albion Terrace and some of the others).

Craven Arms has never really achieved the feel of an urban settlement, however, and except during the autumn sheep sales, when up to 20,000 sheep can be sold in a day and the place bustles with business activity, it can easily appear as an alien Victorian intrusion into the picturesque tranquillity of the south Shropshire countryside. At least it is quickly left behind by travellers on Watling Street (West), who can rejoin the Roman route by travelling west along the B4368 and turning left into Park Lane.

The turning is unpromisingly signposted 'Waste Disposal Site 2½ Miles', but after passing under a narrow railway bridge carrying the Heart of Wales line the road assumes its real character of a quiet country lane. At the end of a stiff climb there are wide views left, from the tower on Callow Hill to the sharply pointed crest of Stoke Wood, which rises above Stokesay Castle, the magnificent stone and half-timbered edifice said to be the least damaged fortified house surviving from the medieval period in Britain. Sadly the castle is out of sight, even from the top of a conveniently situated five-barred gate.

Park Lane continues south as a notably straight minor road, though there are minor deviations to fit in with the local topography. To the east the scarp of View Edge is prominent, but the ground rises slightly to the west and so there are only fleeting glimpses of Rowton, site of another temporary fortlet during the first phase of Roman occupation. Beyond the Rowton crossroads the panorama to the west suddenly comes into view, with an excellent prospect over the broad Clun valley to the rounded and well-wooded Hopton Titterhill and Bedstone Hill.

At the road junction by Crossways Cottage there is scope for a detour to Clungunford, but having sampled this and been disappointed I would recommend the direct walk along the lane to Shelderton, small and nondescript yet with a surprisingly complicated road pattern. Maintain a southerly course, eventually turning right on to a sunken and narrow lane, and after 300 yards take the middle of three gates and proceed along a heavily overgrown bridleway sandwiched between hedges. In places the surface has been roughly repaired with rubble, but the route can hardly be used by more than a handful of vehicles. Now there is a hollow by a huge oak tree, after which the way lies along the left-hand edge of a field. At the far corner a battle through tall bracken only reveals a barbed-wire fence across the right of way.

(opposite top) The view north along the course of the Roman road from the duckpond at Stormer Hall; (bottom) Leintwardine Bridge and the River Teme

There seem to be three choices here: a retreat to the road, and consequently 2 miles of road walking to Leintwardine; exploration of the fields on the right (where there are no rights of way) in an attempt to reach the B4385 nearer to Leintwardine; or perseverance along what is undoubtedly the right of way. Having tried the second alternative I would never do so again – the terrain is difficult and it involves leaving the footpath. In fact perseverance, though it seems a lost cause to begin with, is far better. Once over the illegal barbed wire the way ahead is obvious if overgrown, with a tall hedgerow impressively defining the route for much of the remaining distance to Leintwardine.

Keep to the east of, and above, Marlow Farm and take the increasingly well-marked track alongside the hedgerow to the duckpond north of Stormer Hall, an impressive collection of buildings which the route passes on the left. Then the way lies due south – a spot of waymarking would help – to join the B4385 at the northern edge of Leintwardine, an attractive and surprisingly lively village at the confluence of the Teme and Clun.

Don't miss the Sun Inn, with beer straight from the barrel, wooden benches in a side room, and special prices for regulars. Roman tiles and bricks have been discovered beneath the village church, and indeed the village is largely contained within the ramparts of the Roman fort of Bravonium. This seems to have been constructed in about 160 AD, as a successor to the earliest forts in the central Marches; the quite substantial ramparts can still be seen, especially to the north and west of the village.

Notes

Maps   OS 1:50,000 sheet 137. The 1:25,000 sheet SO47/57 is also useful to sort out the problem south of Shelderton mentioned in the text.
Further reading   Trevor Rowley, *The Shropshire Landscape* (Hodder & Stoughton, 1972); S. C. Stanford, *The Archaeology of the Welsh Marches* (Collins, 1980).
Public transport   Church Stretton has an adequate rail service and there are also buses from Shrewsbury and Hereford (which also pass through Marshbrook). Leintwardine has an afternoon bus to Ludlow on certain days, and a later bus to Bucknell and Knighton (for the Central Wales railway line and connections to Church Stretton).

17

THE FOSSE WAY

Lordswood Farm to Kemble Aerodrome 10 miles/16km

This is an easy walk along a classically straight 'Roman' road over the Cotswold plateau. Now for much of its length a bridleway forming the county boundary between Gloucestershire and Wiltshire, the route is used by farm vehicles and horses in places and can become waterlogged after rain.

Historical Background

The advance of the Roman army through southern England after the invasion in 43 AD was devastatingly rapid, and within five or six years the whole of England south-east of the Jurassic limestone ridge running from Dorset through the Cotswolds to Lincolnshire had been subjugated. But the Welsh tribes (particularly the Silures in South Wales) posed a continuing threat, and so the frontier was strengthened with the construction of forts at regular intervals between Lincoln and Axmouth. Naturally the forts were connected by a defensive frontier road – the Fosse Way.

The Fosse Way was the cornerstone of the early Roman defences, allowing troops to be moved quickly along the frontier to quell outbreaks of resistance. It may even have been intended originally as the permanent boundary of a Roman province which would only have included lowland England. In fact its use as a frontier road was very temporary, for by 49 AD the Roman legions were attacking further west, attempting to crush resistance in the Welsh borders. A new line of forts, including Alcester, Gloucester and Sea Mills (near Bristol) was established and it is thought that the Roman army had all but left the Cotswolds by the end of the first century AD.

The chain of forts along the Fosse Way included those at Bath (Aquae Sulis) and Cirencester (Corinium). Between these two important Roman settlements there would have been smaller forts, probably at Nettleton Shrub, a religious and military site, and White Walls, near Easton Grey – strategically placed to defend the crossing of the River Avon. The walk described below starts just to the north of Nettleton Shrub and passes the site of White Walls.

After the first phase of the Roman occupation, the Cotswolds and the surrounding area quickly developed into the 'granary of Britain', with the

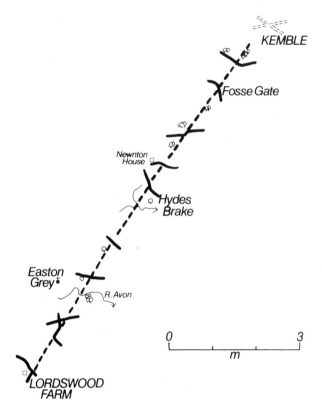

growth of agricultural settlements and the development of a number of prosperous villas in the open countryside (as, for instance, at Long Newnton, north-east of White Walls). The site at White Walls, abandoned by the army, probably took on a new role as a market centre, and it may have continued to fulfil this role until at least the end of Roman rule in the fourth and fifth centuries.

Description of the Route

The Fosse Way heads north-east from the Lordswood Farm crossroads (ST872843) as a very wide green lane, overgrown in places and very badly churned up by a combination of farm vehicles and horses' hooves. Avoiding the worst of the sea of mud can be difficult after rain, and this is certainly a route best walked after a prolonged dry spell.

After half a mile or so the going improves as height is gained and the Fosse Way becomes a true green road rising past a prominent windpump, with the hazy outline of the hamlet of Norton away to the right. The road continues as a wide drift joining the Norton to Easton Grey road, which uses its course for a while but then veers away to the left. Just before this, an inviting field gate on the right indicates a path, but the line of the Roman road here is difficult to follow. In any case the road curving to the left, itself following the course

The view south along the Fosse Way near Norton

of an unimportant Roman branch road which headed off northwards through Easton Grey, offers a better view, across a geese-ridden cottage garden, of the hedgerows marking the line of the Fosse Way.

Turn right at a crossroads after 200 yards and regain the line of the Fosse Way, thickly wooded at this point, after a further 200 yards or so. The way lies down a muddy lane to a rather confined section of the route crossing a minor stream. From here, however, matters improve quickly as the lane rises between high hedgerows as a slightly less muddy brown track. When the top of the hill is reached the lane continues relentlessly north-east, the hedges delimiting its route now reinforced by attractive, though dilapidated, Cotswold drystone walls.

From the hilltop there are wide views left towards Sherston, and right to Foxley, a small village with church, rectory and cottages spaced around a triangular green. Immediately east of Foxley (but over a mile away from the Fosse Way) is Cowage Farm, where a tiny chapel consisting of nave and bellcote is the sole survivor of the medieval settlement of Bremilham.

The well-defined muddy track ends at a gate, where the course of the Fosse Way becomes a sunken holloway descending deeply to the crossing of the River Avon (here flowing east to Malmesbury but eventually curving westwards to Bath and Bristol). The holloway is, however, liberally protected by barbed wire and the path has been diverted slightly to the left to cross the Avon on an attractive three-arched Cotswold-stone bridge.

The Roman road clearly forded the river slightly downstream from the present bridge, and then headed directly up the northern slope of the valley. The Romano-British settlement of White Walls lay to the left of the road, but there are few traces of this in the water meadows. This was an important early Roman site, one of a chain of forts guarding the Fosse Way frontier, and later a significant Romano-British settlement, covering some fifty acres on the south-facing slope of the Avon valley. Eighteenth-century excavations revealed the foundations of walls, a mosaic pavement and a quantity of coins, and more recently pottery, glass and an excellent martingale (part of a harness) with a projecting horse's head have been discovered.

The route rises north-east from the river bridge towards another gate, then becomes confined between high hedgerows again and, after another muddy interlude, reaches the top of the hill. Here an unexpected but welcome concrete strip appears in the middle of the track, offering a firm footing to the next gate, where a substantial farm road joins from the right and the surface improves dramatically. Within 200 yards the B4040 Malmesbury to Sherston road is reached; the excellent Red Bull Inn lies about a mile to the right.

The Roman road still maintains the same north-easterly direction across the B4040 and past Upper Fosse Farm and a prominent and startlingly ugly waterworks. The track now has a gravel base as far as the Shipton Moyne road. The way lies between Shipton Moyne and Brokenborough – two more villages which, following the usual pattern, lie discreetly away from the Fosse Way – with the spire of Malmesbury Abbey mistily visible on the horizon to the right of a notably large field barn.

Beyond a substantial farm and equally substantial duckpond the Fosse Way is well surfaced until a lane bears off across the plateau to the right, leading to Brokenborough. The Fosse itself now continues as a green lane with wide views, typical of the Cotswold dip-slope, to right and left. Suddenly, however, the good track ends and the Roman road plunges down a steep slope as a narrow footpath. At the bottom is a morass, partly created by horses and rogue motorcyclists, but luckily the worst of it can be by-passed through a thicket on the left. After a small stream, easily forded on stepping stones, the Fosse Way resembles an ordinary footpath, narrow and winding.

An attractive bridge carries the path over a much wider stream near Hydes Brake, and at the top of a quite steep climb back to the plateau the character of the Fosse Way changes completely, to a very deeply rutted green lane, as far as the B4014. There are panoramic views to the left now, as far as the imposing seven-bayed façade of Newnton House, built in about 1800 for Thomas White, and the Perpendicular tower of Long Newnton church.

The bridge carrying the Fosse Way over the River Avon near Easton Grey

Between the Fosse Way and Newnton House is the likely site of a fairly large Romano-British settlement, with evidence spread over about an acre, and an adjoining villa, one of many in the fertile Cotswolds. In the same area concentrations of flints on the surface of ploughed fields have been seen as indicating the site of a neolithic settlement.

At another road junction a minor road leading to a disused airfield takes over the line, but where this road bends to the right the Fosse Way keeps straight on yet again, as a wet track skirting the perimeter of the airfield and traversing an eerie landscape of disused sheds and occasional concrete roads. A black water-tower looming ahead adds to the sense of desolation.

Beyond a gate the track merges with and crosses a minor road, then continues as an even more deeply rutted lane, with apparently permanent standing water in some of the deepest ruts. But the going soon improves and the Fosse Way becomes a pleasant, quiet green lane running between lines of mature trees. North from here the remains of the Roman agger are more readily apparent. The embankment is up to 30ft wide and about 2ft high, and the bridleway generally only uses part of the width as it heads for Fosse Gate. At times the way is bounded by extensive rabbit burrows and indeed in places it seems in danger of being undermined.

Bridge over the Fosse Way at Hyde's Brake

At Fosse Gate the junction of the Roman road and a minor lane is clumsy, although the wider line of the Fosse Way – indicated by two lines of hedgerows – continues uninterrupted across the later lane. There is now less than a mile to travel, along a tree-lined avenue and then to the west of a copse, to the point (ST952958) where Kemble aerodrome severs the line and effectively ends a walk which, in traversing the attractive though almost deserted countryside of the Cotswold dip-slope, has demonstrated the unflinching commitment of the Roman road-builders to maintaining a straight alignment wherever possible.

Notes

Maps   OS 1:50,000 sheets 163 and 173.
Further reading   Ivan Margary, *Roman Roads in Britain* (John Baker, 3rd edn. 1973); Graham Webster, *The Roman Invasion of Britain* (Batsford, 1980).
Public transport   Neither start nor finish of the walk is well served by public transport, although with some ingenuity a circular tour can be arranged from Swindon or Chippenham. Hatts Coaches run an excellent service from Chippenham to Malmesbury, calling at Hullavington, 2 miles from Lordswood Farm. Alternatively Sherston, 1½ miles from the start, can be reached from Yate or Malmesbury (Fosseway Coaches). Kemble station, on the Gloucester to Swindon line, is 3 miles from the end of the walk.

18

A COTSWOLD SALTWAY

Bourton-on-the-Hill to Westcote 9 miles/14km

The walk follows part of a saltway known to have been in existence in the eighth century, using footpaths, bridleways and minor lanes linking a series of attractive Cotswold villages and skirting the market and tourist centre of Stow-on-the-Wold.·

Historical Background

Saltways are the most enduring of the Dark Age trackways, and their survival emphasises the importance of salt in the Saxon and medieval economy. Trade routes radiate in all directions from the most important salt-producing centres, notably Northwich in Cheshire and Droitwich in Worcestershire, and many of these routes are still in use as main roads today.

Many Cotswold villages owned salt pits and springs at Droitwich, and so an intricate network of saltways spread across the Vale of Evesham and up into the Cotswolds. The best-known of these climbed the Cotswold scarp above Hailes Abbey, passed close to Northleach and Bibury, and reached Lechdale, the head of navigation on the Thames. But much of this route, which is clearly marked on the OS map, now consists of busy minor roads and is unsuitable for walking.

A more promising alternative for the walker is the saltway which led south from Chipping Campden to Blockley and Stow-on-the-Wold, then followed the western slopes of the Evenlode valley downstream to Widford, finally reaching Bampton on the River Thames. The central section of this saltway (which is referred to in eighth-century documents) no longer exists as a through road, but footpaths and bridleways follow the line across the Cotswold plateau.

Description of the Route

The saltway approached the village of Bourton-on-the-Hill from the north-west along a lane leaving the Blockley road in Bourton Woods. It descended the hill as far as the church (SP175325) by means of the present main road and then veered southwards over the fields to Sezincote. Before tracing its

113

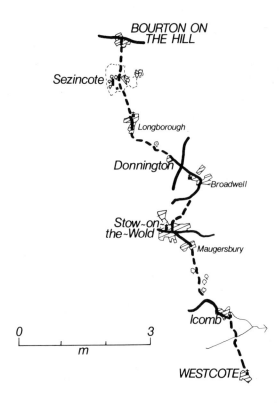

course, however, take a look around Bourton, a quiet place of old stone cottages, with little alleys around the churchyard. The church, originally Norman, has been much restored, and Bourton House is more interesting. This sixteenth-century manor house lies near the foot of the hill and still retains its medieval stone brewhouse, stables and dovecot, although the house itself was remodelled and acquired Ionic pilasters and a classical veneer in the eighteenth century. The Cotswold stone tithe barn, one of the largest in the area with its seven bays and gabled porches, is dated 1570.

Leave Bourton church down the steps at the eastern end of the churchyard, turn right along the road, right again at a telephone box and then left (signposted to Sezincote and Longborough) along a green alley between two cottages. At a gate, keep straight on along the right-hand edge of a field (the ruins of what appears to be a former walled garden are on the left) and maintain the same general direction across fields and through a tree belt to a gate leading into the grounds of Sezincote House.

Sezincote appears in Domesday Book as Cheisnecott ('the gravelly cottage'), but the village which grew here was a casualty of the enclosure movement and depopulation, and by 1638 the church was in ruins. The big house remained, however, and in 1805 Sir Charles Cockerell began to remodel it in an oriental style, with a Mogul dome rising above the eleven bays of the house, which is faced with an artificially stained orange stone.

114

Sezincote, where the Prince Regent stayed in 1807, provided the inspiration for the Brighton Pavilion.

The line of the saltway passes through Sezincote Park at a respectful distance from the house, skirting the attractive wood-fringed lake and then climbing to a yellow waymark painted on the tallest of three trees at the crest of a small hill. The route lies south, with a pheasant-infested copse to the right, through an ancient kissing-gate and across a track, and then straight on over the fields to Longborough, already visible in the middle distance. A pleasant, classically Cotswold village, with warm stone cottages and the welcoming Coach and Horses crowding around a small triangular green, Longborough is larger than it appears at first sight, and with its shops, post office and primary school is clearly a thriving community.

Take the road to Stow, passing a picturesque row of cottages beyond a grassy bank bright with daffodils in spring, but after a few hundred yards fork left along a 'no through road'. This quickly peters out into a bridleway making for Donnington, across rough pasture described as the 'saltemor' in 1277. Donnington, no more than a hamlet, is approached past an ostentatiously big house with a marvellous view over the Evenlode valley. There was a 'salt strete' here – possibly the lane to Broadwell – as early as the eighth century.

Longborough

The lane crosses the Fosse Way, here the A429, and heads past the site of a Roman villa to the village of Broadwell. At the western end of the village are the church, with its Perpendicular tower and an impressive array of seventeenth-century table tombs in the churchyard, and the Georgian manor house. The rest of the village is grouped around an extraordinarily large green; on one corner is the Fox Inn, selling excellent real ales from the Donnington Brewery (which lies a mile or so west of the hamlet of Donnington) and an adventurous range of food.

South of the Fox is the road to Stow, and ½ mile along this a path (later a narrow lane) leads more directly south-west to the town, passing on the way a large stone trough – one of the wells, fed by a spring, from which Stow's water supply once had to be carried. Follow Well Lane, as it is now called, and then turn right into Parson's Corner to discover the market square of Stow-on-the-Wold, a new town of the twelfth century which became a thriving market centre but is now unashamedly wedded to the tourist trade. The result is a busy town, thronged with tourists in summer, suffering from a surfeit of antique shops.

The market place is dominated by the Victorian town hall and a remarkable collection of old inns, many dating from the time when the fairs and markets brought trade and prosperity; at one time the Kings Arms was regarded as the best inn between London and Worcester. The most attractive building is St Edward's House, dating from the early years of the eighteenth century. The parish church, said to be ruinous in 1657 but quickly restored, stands aloof from the market place and can be reached along one of the alleys which run off the square.

Follow the Oxford road (A436) out of the town as far as the Bell Inn, then take the lane signposted to Maugersbury, founded in 708 and the parent settlement of Stow. Fortunately the lane is accompanied by a footpath as far as the village, notable for its seventeenth-century farmhouses and Crescent House, built in 1800 by Edmund Chamberlayne. Originally a row of workers' cottages, with a Sunday school and communal oven in the middle, the Crescent House is now a single dwelling.

The saltway continues southwards, plunging steeply down from Maugersbury along a lane signposted to Oxleaze Farm, with fine views ahead of the prominent ridge of Icomb Hill. At the bottom of the hill is a small stream and the trackbed of the Chipping Norton to Cheltenham railway. The way then lies quite steadily upwards past the substantial complex of farm buildings at

(*opposite top*) Cotswold stone walling and a stepped alley leading to the church at Bourton on the Hill; (*bottom*) Well Lane, Stow: one of the wells which provided water for medieval Stow-on-the-Wold

Oxleaze and along a baked-mud track to the Icomb road, close to a rather ill-defined and possibly unfinished hill-fort in a tangle of ditches and undergrowth.

Now the saltway descends into the exquisite small village of Icomb, with its honey-coloured cottages and rather more sombre church. Icomb Place, built in 1420 by Sir John Blaket, retains a medieval courtyard, an Early Tudor doorway and a number of fifteenth-century features. A pre-Conquest charter refers to Icomb's 'saltuelle', providing yet further documentary evidence of the antiquity of this route.

The way lies to the right of the church, snaking round between this and the farm, then over the stile and along the lane for a few paces before crossing the farmyard and dropping down past an artificial lake to the Westcote Brook, a tributary of the Evenlode, the river which has been a constant companion, albeit at arm's length, for much of the walk. Keep to the path as it continues south past Gawcombe to the village of Westcote, noted for its medieval manor house and views over the Evenlode valley to Wychwood Forest.

Westcote (SP220206) is as good a place as any to leave the saltway, which is now represented by the lanes linking the villages of Westcote, Idbury, and Fifield on their bench above the Evenlode. Pleasant though the countryside is around here, the quality of the walking inevitably suffers as the traffic increases. These lanes previously formed the main road between Stow and Burford, but the turnpike road along the ridge superseded them in 1756. The saltway lay to the east of Burford, crossing the River Windrush at Widford and finally reaching the middle Thames south of Bampton.

Notes

Maps   OS 1:50,000 sheets 151 and 163. Alternatively, the 1in Cotswold Tourist Map covers the route all on one sheet, but the rights of way are more difficult to follow.
Further reading   G. R. Crosher, *Along the Cotswold Ways* (Cassell, 1976); Josceline Finsberg, *The Cotswolds* (Eyre Methuen, 1977).
Public transport   Bourton lies 2 miles west of Moreton-in-Marsh railway station; Westcote is 3 miles from Kingham station. Both of these stations are on the London to Worcester line, and can be used to make a 14 mile (22km) 'circular' walk.

19

VIA DEVANA (WOOL STREET)

Horseheath to Addenbrooke's Hospital, Cambridge 11 miles/18km

Part of the Roman road from Colchester to Ermine Street, the so-called Via Devana, has been abandoned for centuries between Haverhill and Cambridge, having been superseded by the lower valley road. Remarkably, however, it has survived as a green lane (sometimes no more than a narrow footpath) running for miles across the pleasantly undulating open countryside of south-east Cambridgeshire.

Historical Background

Once quite an important Roman road, the so-called Via Devana has been progressively reduced in status for much of its journey between Haverhill and Cambridge. The main route between the towns has moved gradually to the south-west, first into the valley of the Linton Cam and then to the far slopes in places, as the valley villages have been by-passed.

The Romans built the road as part of a cross-country link between Colchester and Ermine Street, passing through Haverhill, Cambridge (Duroliponte, apparently meaning 'the walled town near a swampy river') and Godmanchester. Although another road branches off from Ermine Street, leading towards the Fosse Way at Leicester (see the Gartree Road chapter) it does not seem to have penetrated further west and so the notion expressed in the later title, Via Devana ('the road to Chester'), is purely fanciful. Nevertheless the name has become attached to the road in south-east Cambridgeshire, and it forms a useful description as long as it is recognised that the title was never used by the Romans, and indeed was concocted as late as the eighteenth century.

From the moment the Romans abandoned it the story of the road appears to have been one of unremitting decline. Apart from one or two small Romano-British settlements near Bartlow and Linton there is little evidence of Roman colonisation of the area, and so there was no need for the Saxons to maintain the straight road on the plateau. Instead, they settled the river valleys, and the lanes connecting the villages of Babraham, the Abingtons, Hildersham and Linton developed into the main through route.

Indeed, not only was the Roman road allowed to fall into disuse, it actually became a place of some danger – its second name, Wool Street, began life as Wolvestreet, 'the road infested with wolves'. Later, there were no great droves of sheep or cattle to reinvigorate the road (the chalk grasslands of the eighteenth century were completely converted to arable in the first few decades of the nineteenth century) and so the Roman road has survived as a narrow green path between luxuriant hedges, a complete and welcome contrast to the wide open spaces of the massive Cambridgeshire cornfields.

Description of the Route

In an ideal world this walk would start in Haverhill's straight and obviously Roman High Street and continue north-west to Cambridge. Sadly, there is a 2 mile gap in the footpath network between Haverhill and Horseheath, and so the best place to start is now on the county boundary to the east of Horseheath Park, at TL636472.

The walk quickly recovers from this unpromising start, following the notably direct course of the Roman road through the low hills towards Cambridge. Via Devana runs to the south of Hare Wood, and at this point the Roman agger or embankment is still visible as a foundation for the path. Then, as a rather ill-defined footpath, it keeps to the south side of a very large field before crossing a minor road between Horseheath, a frontier village near the highest point of the valley road, and Streetly End, whose name reflects its proximity to the Roman road.

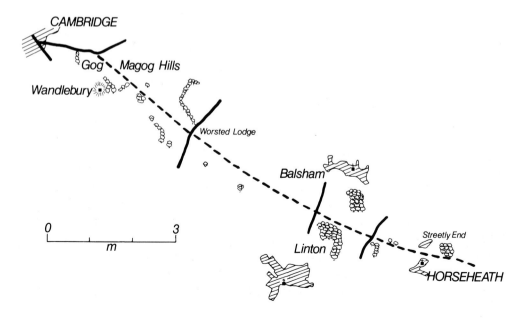

The main street of Linton

The same is true of Streetly Hall, reached along a stretch of the Roman road which has degenerated into a narrow and overgrown path. One of a number of isolated moated farmsteads on the plateau, it was not mentioned in Domesday Book but is listed in the *Inquisitio Eliensis* of the same date. (Yen Hall, a mile or so north, makes its documentary debut as early as 974 AD.) There is no difficulty in following the way through a copse and then downhill across a dry ditch to the Mark's Grave crossing, and on the far side of this road the Roman route widens into a substantial, somewhat rutted track. The view to the right on my journey included a prominent water-tower in front of Balsham, and the billowing grey clouds associated with stubble-burning.

Continue along the track on the north side of Borley Wood, with the Roman agger conspicuous again and the road it supported now represented by a delightful green lane. On the right a path leads in the direction of Balsham, a large village which now has a leavening of Cambridge commuters. The church contains a large Anglo-Saxon grave cover and fine fourteenth-century rood-loft and screen.

Wool Street, now less enclosed, maintains its westerly course along the left-hand edge of a field to cross the B1052 a mile north of Linton, largest of the villages in the vicinity and with a main street whose shops and pubs hint

121

at even greater prosperity in former times. There were regular markets and fairs near the Shepherd's Hall in Market Lane from the thirteenth century until 1860; away from the main street the over-restored church, the late medieval timber-framed Guildhall and a thatched cottage form a pleasant group.

To the west of the B1052 the Roman road is less spacious, with luxuriant hedgerows full of blackberries crowding in on the path, which is itself churned up in places by the passage of horses. The route overlooks the valley of the Linton Cam, separated from it by the immense cornfields around Chilford Hall. The countryside here resembles a Canadian prairie, and the course of Via Devana with its enclosing hedges brings a welcome oasis of colour into a monotone landscape. And the way is important not just visually but for nature conservation too: it carries a rich grassland flora and provides a refuge for animals and birds in a landscape where the emphasis on open space has resulted in a lack of cover and a loss of variety.

Go straight across the Hildersham road, on to a stretch which has pretensions to cart-track status but is bounded by hedges which press in so closely that anything more ambitious than single-file walking is problematical. The Roman road dips slightly, then rises again past Gunner's Hall, by-passing the Abingtons – two picturesque villages with thatched cottages nestling close to the village churches (Great Abington's church can be approached via a stone causeway leading from the Linton Cam).

The green lane now approaches the A11, the modern successor to the Romanised Icknield Way, meeting it at Worsted Lodge, whose name is reputedly a corrupted form of Wolvestreet. Further east the main road crosses Fleam Dyke, which extends for 3 miles and was probably constructed in the early Saxon period to block passage along the Icknield Way. Just beyond Worsted Lodge a lane drops down into Babraham, where the church lies in the garden of the hall, itself a Victorian reconstruction of an Elizabethan manor house. As at Linton and the Abingtons the original main street ran east–west, rising from a ford on the Linton Cam, and the later development of the road along the valley caused a realignment of the main focus of the village.

A straight green lane on the Roman agger, here about 36ft wide and a couple of feet high, runs north–west from Worsted Lodge, passing the burial mound on Copley Hill, submerged in a beech spinney. In another ¼ mile it enters another wood, and a signpost here points the way along a straight enclosed path to the Iron Age hill-fort at Wandlebury. The detour is highly recommended; to make sure of arriving at Wandlebury, bear right in front of a house, then left across woodland, keeping generally to a south-westerly direction.

The enclosed, tree-shaded course of Via Devana in the Gog Magog Hills

Wandlebury is the most impressive and largest of the Iron Age hill-forts in the area, and yet it was once far more impressive, prior to its partial destruction in the eighteenth century. Excavation has indicated that it was originally constructed in the third century BC, and that it was strengthened some two hundred years later, possibly as a defence against the Belgae. The ditches and ramparts are almost 1,000ft in diameter, and are now heavily overgrown with a mixture of beeches and other trees. A mansion was built inside the fort in the eighteenth century, but this has since been demolished and is now represented by its stable block, crowned with a clock tower. The whole site was bought by the Cambridge Preservation Society in 1954 and it now forms a valuable public open space.

Return to the Roman road and turn left, following what is now a cart-track enclosed by thick hedges. The track rises slightly as it breasts the Gog Magog Hills, with views towards Cambridge which are somewhat marred by the

Inside the hill-fort at Wandlebury: the stable block is the only survivor of the eighteenth-century mansion

towers of Addenbrooke's Hospital and other recent building. There is a slight kink where the track joins the Fulbourn to Red Cross road (the parish boundary shows the true course), then Via Devana is represented by the road down to Red Cross. This stretch of road was known as Wort's Causeway, after William Wort who instituted its improvement in the eighteenth century, but it follows the Roman line down to the A1307 at Red Cross, next to Addenbrooke's Hospital (TL470551). Via Devana now leads straight along the main road into Cambridge.

Notes

Map OS 1:50,000 sheet 154.
Further reading Norman Scarfe, *Cambridgeshire: A Shell Guide* (Faber & Faber, 1983); Christopher Taylor, *The Cambridgeshire Landscape* (Hodder & Stoughton, 1973).
Public transport Haverhill has three buses on weekdays from Audley End station and ten buses (three on Sunday) from Cambridge, calling at Horseheath Green. Addenbrooke's Hospital has regular bus services, including the Haverhill buses – so that a round trip is easily planned.

20

PEDDARS WAY

Castle Acre to Holme next the Sea 20 miles/32km

One of the longest walks in the book, this is also one of the easiest, since it involves virtually no climbing, and it is eminently possible to complete it in one day. It traces part of the course of the Roman road from Colchester to Lincoln, and apart from a little road walking at each end it consists of an · uninterrupted green lane by-passing attractive villages as it strikes north to the sea.

Historical Background

Peddars Way, one of the most striking Roman roads both on the ground and on the Ordnance Survey map, which it dominates as it passes through the otherwise virtually deserted countryside of north-west Norfolk, was probably of no great strategic importance in Roman times. It seems to have originated as a native trackway and to have been Romanised as part of the route between Colchester and Lincoln, but it lay well inside the Roman province and may have functioned chiefly as a trade route.

Nevertheless the Romans lavished a good deal of time and effort on the road. The agger on which the road was made is conspicuously well preserved in many places, yet this is a feature which is absent from most other Roman roads in East Anglia. Excavations near to the River Thet (south of the section described below) showed Peddars Way to be a 16ft wide causeway constructed of packed flints topped by fine gravel. The agger often cuts a much wider swathe across the countryside, and near Fring reaches a width of 45ft.

At Castle Acre, where Peddars Way crosses the River Nar and an east–west Roman road (the eastern continuation of the Fen Causeway) there was a Roman fort, and a similar defensive settlement could be expected at Holme next the Sea, where the Roman road reaches the Wash. Clearly this was the southern landing point for a ferry crossing – a time-consuming and difficult journey which will have severely limited the use of Peddars Way as a through route. Nowadays it does perform that function, as part of a designated long-distance footpath (Peddars Way and Norfolk Coast Path), and between Shepherd's Bush, north of Castle Acre, and Ringstead it offers a magnificent walk along an unfrequented green lane.

125

Description of the Route

The first problem is to get out of Castle Acre — not because there are any difficulties in route-finding but because there is so much of interest in the village, much of it rather hidden from view and therefore creating even more of a visual shock when it is discovered. Start at the castle, south-east of the village centre. The earthworks are undoubtedly tremendously impressive, although it is perhaps overstating the case to say, as some have, that they are the finest castle earthworks in England. The motte is over 100ft high and is surmounted by the substantial remains of the curtain wall. The earthworks of the inner bailey cover around 15 acres, and the village is built inside the outer bailey.

The Bailey Gate, dating from the thirteenth century and topped by two circular towers, separates the castle area from the present village green (Stocks Green), with its shops and pubs — notably the Ostrich Inn known for

The motte of Castle Acre castle

Castle Acre Priory

its real ales. West from Stocks Green is the church of St James, with its imposing Perpendicular architecture, and further west still, on the slopes above the River Nar, are the magnificent ruins of the Cluniac priory founded in 1090 by William de Warennes. The remains include the west front, with its tiered arcades, the twelfth-century south-west tower and the much later Prior's Lodging.

Less obvious visually are the reminders of much earlier settlement in Castle Acre. It seems clear that there was a Romano-British settlement here, probably associated with a fort at the junction of Roman roads. After the decline of Roman rule the early Saxons also colonised the site, important strategically as a river crossing, and their cemetery, where numerous cremation urns have been discovered, was situated between Castle Acre and West Acre.

Peddars Way leaves Castle Acre in a northerly direction (from TF817153) as an unclassified but rather busy road to which there is no obvious alternative. After an uneventful 2½ miles the road bends right by an OS triangulation pillar (298ft/91m above sea-level) at Shepherd's Bush. Now, at last, the real walking can begin, along a cart-track within a wide green strip (the successor to the embankment of the Roman road, which can still be seen in places) cutting across the countryside.

Delightful though it is to escape from the traffic on to the rough lane north of Shepherd's Bush, I still have no hesitation in recommending a detour along the country road going north-east from near Fieldbarn Plantation to the exquisite village of Great Massingham. Towards the south end is a small pond, liberally supplied with ducks and surrounded by fine examples of vernacular architecture. The fifteenth-century tower of the village church is well in view, and to the north is a second and much larger pond.

The route of Peddars Way lies about a mile to the west, traversing gently undulating countryside which is almost completely devoid of settlement of any kind. Cross the A148 with care, follow a minor road for a hundred yards or so and then continue in the same direction along a marvellous green lane

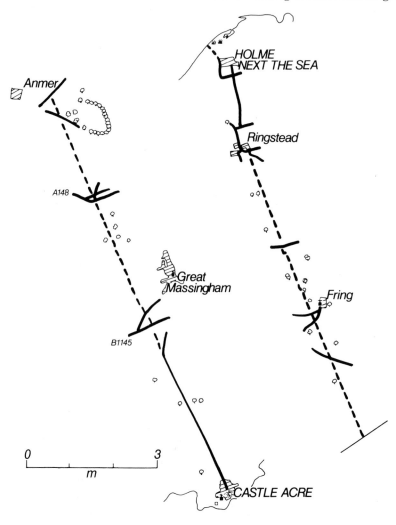

passing a number of barrows before intersecting with the road to Anmer. It is worth considering another detour here, although there is a very private and almost unwelcoming feel to the estate village of Anmer (part of the Sandringham estate) and its church in the grounds of the hall.

North of the Anmer road the green lane, now flanked by trees to the right, continues inexorably towards the sea. The route of Peddars Way is unflinchingly straight, disregarding little climbs across the low ridges characteristic of the open country east of Sandringham. One consequence of these rises is tremendous views, especially eastwards, from a succession of vantage points.

From one such vantage point the church and hamlet of Fring stand out in the well-wooded landscape around the headwaters of the Heacham river. Only ¼ mile from Peddars Way, the hamlet is well worth a visit. There is a fine view of the church from a picturesque little bridge across the brook running through the hamlet; the hall is modern. Peddars Way is here a classic example of a relict green lane enclosed by hedgerows, though as it crosses the Heacham valley it is forced to deviate from a dead straight line for a while.

Sedgeford, to the left of the way, has an attractive yellow-brick Queen Anne hall and a church with a Norman round tower surmounted by an octagonal top storey of rather later vintage. Now a quiet village with few facilities, in 1841 it had three shoemakers, three grocers, three drapers, two blacksmiths, a carpenter and a bricklayer (who also kept a beerhouse), two tailors, a schoolmaster, a baker and a basket-maker.

Peddars Way crosses the B1454 at Littleport, east of Sedgeford, continues on its standard course for ¼ mile, then takes a slight diversion where it crosses a railway line. The true course has been lost in the next field, but the alternative route lies only a hundred yards or so to the east, and the original line is quickly regained past a wood marking the parish boundary between Sedgeford and Ringstead.

Shortly after the wood has been negotiated, the Roman road begins the descent to the sea, which increasingly becomes the dominant feature of the northern horizon. At first the route is marked by another length of green lane, but it degenerates into a yellow-brown track on the outskirts of Ringstead, and alongside a suburban-type ribbon development it becomes a narrow metalled road. The road from Docking commandeers the line for a hundred yards, then the true line of Peddars Way continues straight across at a crossroads. However, this route is no longer a through road and so it is necessary to turn left and follow the road through Ringstead village.

Ringstead once had two churches, but St Peter's has long been disused and now only the tower survives, sited somewhat incongruously in the garden of

Hall Farm. St Andrew's, at the top of the hill, has fared rather better although it was heavily restored by the Victorians. Ringstead Downs, to the west, is a picturesque chalk valley preserved by the Norfolk Naturalists' Trust, with a chalybeate spring close to Barrett Ringstead Farm.

The way out of Ringstead, along the road (named Peddars Way North) to Holme next the Sea, passes a disused windmill but is actually well to the east of the true course of the Roman road, which is indicated now by the lane, further north, forming the parish boundary of Holme and Old Hunstanton. This lane (eventually to be incorporated in the official long-distance footpath) can be seen where it reaches the A149, and its northward continuation, a surfaced lane, can be walked past Beach Cottage down to the sea (TF694440) and the end of the walk at the point where the Roman ferries must have set out across the Wash on their way to Lincolnshire.

Notes

Map   OS 1:50,000 sheet 132.

Further reading   David Kennett, *A Guide to the Norfolk Way* (Constable, 1983).

Accommodation   For those wishing to make a very early start from Castle Acre the Ostrich Inn is recommended.

Public transport   Castle Acre can easily be reached by bus from Kings Lynn and Swaffham. Buses from Hunstanton along the coast road to Wells-next-the-Sea and points east pass through Holme next the Sea.

(*opposite*) One of the Massingham village ponds. In the background is the church of St Mary

21

A MEDIEVAL ROAD
IN CAMBRIDGESHIRE

Sawtry to Wansford 14 miles/22km

Although this is not the easiest of walks to follow it has the distinction of tracing a subsequently abandoned medieval route across the fen-edge landscape south-west of Peterborough – a landscape where not only the road but also the villages it connected have suffered from decline, to the extent that some of them are now deserted.

Historical Background

During the period of Roman rule in Britain the main road to the north was Ermine Street, which ran from Godmanchester to Alconbury Hill, Durobrivae and Lincoln. Following the Roman withdrawal the road fell into disuse, possibly because of the collapse of the bridge over the River Nene at Durobrivae, and traffic was diverted westwards, away from the fen edge.

On this higher ground two roads vied for importance. One led from Alconbury Hill through Upton, Ogerston and Elton to Wansford; later it was used as a drove route and it is sometimes called the Bullock Road. The other – whose route we shall be tracing – lay between the Bullock Road and the abandoned Ermine Street. It forms the main streets of the villages of Sawtry and Glatton, then runs through Caldecote, Morborne and Haddon to Durobrivae, before turning north-west above the Nene valley to Wansford. Later, these medieval ways declined in importance, and Ermine Street returned to favour as a turnpike road (and nowadays a dual-carriageway trunk road).

In part the decline of the roads simply reflected decline in the countryside through which they passed, for most of the villages on the route of the Sawtry to Wansford road are pale shadows of their medieval counterparts. Washingley was deserted by the sixteenth century, Caldecote withered away much later, and Glatton, Morborne and Denton all exhibit the characteristics of shrunken villages, with empty spaces marking the sites of vanished houses. Now the road itself is reduced to paths for much of its length, and indeed it too is in danger of disappearing altogether in some places.

Description of the Route

Begin the walk at Toll Bar Cottages (TL177823), where the medieval road left Ermine Street and nowadays a footpath angles away from the A1. Beyond Whitehall Farm on the left are the few remains of Sawtry Judith, a manor once held by William the Conqueror's niece, the Countess Judith, but later given to the monks of Sawtry Abbey and apparently abandoned in the fifteenth century. The sites of several roads, together with a manor house and some house platforms, have been identified but the settlement is now partly covered by Archer's Wood.

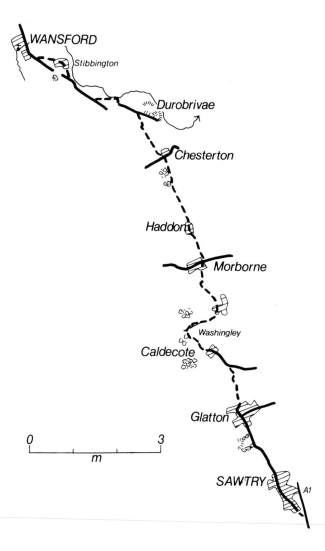

The footpath from Toll Bar Cottages soon joins a minor road leading to Green End, once a separate hamlet with cottages arranged around a common but now merely part of the fen-edge village of Sawtry. A big but not especially attractive village with a Victorian church and little of architectural merit, Sawtry has now expanded beyond the street plan dictated by the medieval route which formed its main street, this latter circumstance giving an indication of the early date at which the alternative to the Roman road was formed.

A minor road indicates the medieval way past Middlemarsh Farm to Glatton, a prosperous village with a good deal of well-preserved thatch and a highly attractive church. Yet the village was once much bigger, as the gaps between the remaining houses on the north–south medieval road, which as at Sawtry formed the main axis, indicate.

To the north of Glatton the medieval road is disused (apart from one small stretch) for miles, and if only the path was preserved it would make a fine walk along the edge of the fen country. Sadly, the through route has been neglected and it now takes determination to walk it – though, since it is a right of way throughout, there can be no doubt about the propriety of doing so.

The first hint of problems to come occurs on the northern fringe of Glatton; where the road bends left, the way to Denton leaves on the right, as a 'road used as a public path' according to the OS map. Yet although the way is clear for pedestrians, it is hardly accurate to describe it as a road, since it is narrow and overgrown. Nevertheless it is reasonably obvious as a footpath across the fields to Denton, another hamlet which was once a fully-fledged village.

Only ½ mile to the north along the medieval way lies Caldecote, an even more interesting example of the decline of the English village. The Black Death in 1349 resulted in severe disruption: three years later many houses were still ruinous, the mill was derelict and the plague was still rife. But Caldecote survived – 'the Town' is prominent on a map of the village in 1753 – and it was only in the nineteenth century that desertion finally took place. Now there are a few modern bungalows, but the tiny church is in a desperate state, abandoned and soon to be engulfed by shrubs and nettles.

The medieval road takes the lane leading past Caldecote church and between pollarded trees to Manor Farm, a substantial complex with tower and stable block. Now the problems really start, for although the map is peppered with footpaths in this vicinity, the reality is very different. The way clearly lies through the farmyard on the right, but at the far corner the vast expanse of an untracked cornfield meets the eye. Tractor marks through the corn are hopelessly misleading and a compass course along the line of the path through the field to Washingley is recommended; the detailed map makes the right of way obvious.

The abandoned parish church of Caldecote

The way emerges at Hall Farm, where 'private' notices abound but a bridleway exists. The site of the deserted medieval village of Washingley is immediately north of the minor road, and the house platforms and sunken village streets can readily be discerned. In 1279 there were forty-two tenants here, but by 1332 the number was down to twenty-seven. In the mid-fifteenth century the manor was eligible for 67 per cent tax relief and by 1534 the church was in ruins. The village and its mixed economy had gone, replaced by sheep pasture tended by only a handful of labourers.

The medieval road is now represented by a footpath north-east from Washingley, but again it is more evident on the map than on the ground; there is certainly a strong case for more signposting in this area. After ½ mile it emerges at the end of the village street of Folksworth (recently much enlarged as a dormitory settlement for Greater Peterborough), then, signposted for once, heads for Morborne, entering this scattered village along the drive of Manor Farm.

Morborne's church is another which is suffering from neglect, partly because of a lack of parishioners, for this is another village which is just a

135

shadow of its former self as a result of the nineteenth-century drift to the towns. And the landscape here is memorable only for the wrong reasons – an ugly television transmitter to the west, and a distant view of the Whittlesey brickworks chimneys to the east.

Thankfully there is a very obvious track northwards from Morborne, yet even this becomes less well defined as it nears Haddon, and the footpath on the left leading to a lane south of the church is more easily traced than the direct line. Take the lane running through the village, partially deserted and still mainly an agricultural community despite the nearness of Peterborough, but where the Elton road bears left take the track to the right. There is (again) no signpost but there is a gate for pedestrians next to one for vehicles labelled 'Mortar Pitts'. The track across the cornfield is reasonably clear on its way past an OS pillar to Chesterton Upper Lodge and a lane leading to Chesterton itself.

Chesterton (literally 'settlement by a Roman station') takes its name from its proximity to the Roman town of Durobrivae, less than a mile away across the fields. The town was established at the point where Ermine Street crossed the River Nene, and in addition to defending the bridge it acted as the focus of a remarkably large Roman pottery industry, with kilns and workshops arranged between Durobrivae and Water Newton.

Cottage near Wansford Church

The Nene bridge at Wansford

The faint outline of the banks and ditches enclosing the 44 acre Roman town can be glimpsed from the point where the Chesterton footpath reaches the A1, but the site itself is inaccessible. The medieval road now follows the dual-carriageway A1 to Wansford – hardly a pleasant prospect for the walker – but after a short stretch to Water Newton most of this arid road walking can be avoided. Water Newton's attractive church lies on the banks of the River Nene (hence the first element of the village name), and to the east the lock-keeper's cottage and eighteenth-century water mill complete an attractive group.

A mixture of path and road walking leads to Stibbington, a classically pretty stone-built village with a fine Jacobean hall, and finally to Wansford via the former Great North Road. A street village aligned along the road, Wansford gives the impression of having tried to become important, but it has merely become a quietly picturesque backwater instead. In the eighteenth century it became a port on the River Nene, importing coal and grain and sending Ketton stone downstream, but the wharves fell into disuse around 1880 and now only pleasure craft can be seen from Wansford bridge (TL075992), a fine structure which houses in one of its arches a stone marking the former boundary between the county of Huntingdon and the Soke of Peterborough.

Notes

Map   OS 1:50,000 sheet 142 covers the whole walk, but the 1:25,000 sheets TL08/18 and TL09/19 are strongly recommended since they show the path in relation to field boundaries.

Further reading   Peter Bigmore, *The Bedfordshire & Huntingdonshire Landscape* (Hodder & Stoughton, 1979); Christopher Taylor, *Roads and Tracks of Britain* (Dent, 1979).

Public transport   Sawtry has a roughly hourly bus service from Peterborough. Wansford has five buses a day from Peterborough, and there are also steam trains in summer.

22

GARTREE ROAD

Leicester (Stoughton Road) to Glooston 10 miles/16km

Gartree Road is the traditional name for the Roman road which departed south-east from the fort at Leicester (Ratae Coritanorum) to Stanion, near Corby, and then probably continued to meet Ermine Street at Alconbury Hill. From Stoughton Road, on the outskirts of Leicester, to Glooston this is an excellent walk across open countryside; further on the rights of way are discontinuous.

Historical Background

Gartree Road was never in the first division of Roman roads in Britain; it seems to have been constructed as a link road connecting the temporary frontier of the early Roman province, the Fosse Way, with more secure territory in the south-east. It could have been used to transport troops to the frontier, but was more probably established to act as a local supply route in peacetime, after the frontier had quickly and decisively been moved to the north-west.

The notion that Gartree Road formed part of a through route from Colchester to Chester – the so-called Via Devana – is almost certainly incorrect. The section between Colchester and Godmanchester certainly existed (and the fine walk along what is now a green lane between Haverhill and Cambridge has already been described) but the connection between Ermine Street and Gartree Road has not definitely been established, and there is no evidence at all for a road through the inhospitable Charnwood Forest, north-west of Leicester.

The Saxons appear to have made little use of the route as a through way, though since parts of the Gartree Road were used as parish boundaries it clearly retained some significance. Generally, however, the road was abandoned with the exception of certain stretches connecting villages, and it has remained in this state ever since. Now it consists of a mixture of old country lanes, roads revived at the time of the enclosure movement, and stretches of bridleway and green lane subjected to varying degrees of use and disuse – an attractive historical patchwork for the present-day rambler.

Description of the Route

The route proper, largely avoiding suburban Leicester, starts at the junction of London Road and Stoughton Road (SK607022), but the same point can be reached on foot by tracing the line of the Roman road from the city centre. To do this, start at Pocklington's Walk and travel south-east along the pedestrian route known as New Walk, first laid out in 1785 and described by Pevsner as unique in England. Some original houses survive at the town end of this walk, although there have been a number of intrusions of more modern, and often sub-standard, buildings.

Nevertheless New Walk survives as a tree-lined pedestrian precinct right to the top of the hill, where Victoria Park has to be crossed. The Roman road is now barely traceable through the affluent suburb of Stoneygate, but it emerges on Stoughton Road and can be approximately followed along Gartree Lane (the actual route lay slightly further north, across the golf course, and a footpath coincides with it for part of the way) to Stoughton Grange, which was one of Leicester Abbey's most important farms in the early medieval period.

Here the way lies straight ahead (the village of Stoughton, ½ mile to the left, has a church with a fine crocketed spire and a few old cottages, but nothing of compelling interest) past a minor airfield and then down a sharp hill into what remains of Great Stretton. Twenty years ago, on my first visit,

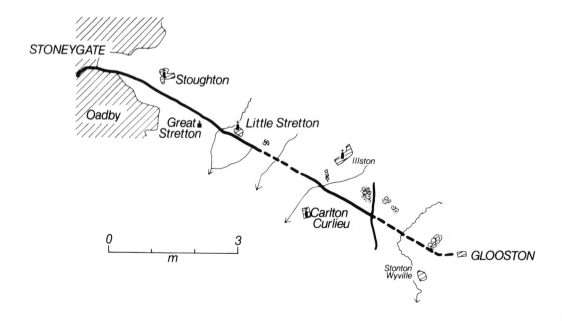

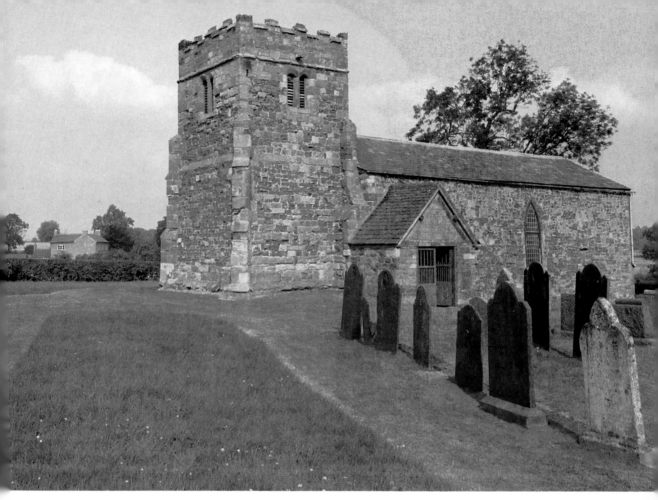

The church of St Giles, one of the few tangible remains of the deserted village of Great Stretton

this deserted village site struck me as eerie and forlorn; now the churchyard is manicured and the effect is somehow much less impressive.

The present settlement consists merely of a large farm and an ironstone church with a squat tower. But in the field to the south of the church are the sunken holloways and raised house platforms delineating the substantial medieval village of Great Stretton – a village large enough to boast a moated manor house. Even in Elizabethan times there were fifteen households here, but decline set in quickly and a hundred years later even the church was in ruins.

Gartree Road continues south-east as a country lane, but after crossing the River Sence the modern road zigzags right and left. The straight course of the Roman road, abandoned for no apparent reason, can just be discerned. The road by-passes Little Stretton, with its Georgian manor house and pleasant group of eighteenth-century farms and cottages, and after a further ½ mile peters out at a crossroads.

The view south-east along the green lane forming Gartree Road south of Little Stretton

The way ahead is marked 'unsuitable for motors', and thankfully it is. This is a marvellous green lane, descending between hedgerows to cross a small stream. On the way down, through gaps in the hedges, the churches at King's Norton and Gaulby, the former described by Pevsner as one of the most remarkable of the Early Gothic Revival churches in England, are prominent on the left.

The Roman road climbs gently from the stream, with intermittent signs of the Roman embankment, to a junction with the Illston to Burton Overy road, then presses on as a metalled lane passing Carlton Curlieu manor house. The lane deviates slightly to pass in front of the house, a solid grey seventeenth-century country house set well away from its village. At the next crossroads the way lies, as usual, straight ahead along a very narrow lane within a wide green enclosure.

Beyond the B6047 Gartree Road is signposted as a field road to Glooston. For about a hundred yards it is roughly surfaced, but this is for the benefit of

Shangton Grange, whose access track bears off to the left. Now the description of 'field road' becomes very apt as the Roman route dips steeply down along the left-hand edge of a field to a five-barred gate. Wide views ahead and to the right include Langton Caudle, with its fox coverts, and the strangely shaped Crossburrow Hill.

The aforementioned gate proved especially difficult to open when I last attempted the feat. Once through it, the route is much less obvious across the next field, although tractor marks lead the eye to a second gate, after which the Gartree Road becomes confined between overgrown hedges for a short distance, then emerges again at the edge of a very large field. Once again the left-hand hedgerow is the key, and the path curves slightly left as it crosses a wide, shallow valley and climbs the opposite slopes.

At a complex junction of tracks there is a choice of enticing diversions. To the left are the wide-open spaces of deserted countryside around the lost village of Noseley, while to the right lies Stonton Wyville. Here there is a wonderfully overgrown, overcrowded churchyard thick with yew trees and slanting shafts of sunlight; sadly the little church was appallingly over-restored by the Victorians and nowadays has a musty, neglected air to it. At least it seems to be kept open at present – it was locked when I was there in 1967 – and it is worth penetrating the gloom to see the Brudenell monuments, the oldest dating from 1590.

Carlton Curlieu manor house

The Brudenells also held the manor of Glooston, which lies only a mile or so away from the junction of tracks which prompted the diversion to Stonton Wyville. Beyond Stonton Wood the present green lane no longer follows the course of the Roman road, which (unattended by public rights of way) passes south of Glooston and Cranoe and heads for the Welland valley.

The field road, wide and green, passes the site of the moated medieval manor house and then forms an attractive approach to Glooston (SP751958), although derelict farm buidlings on the left take away some of the appeal of the abrupt entrance into the village street. Beyond the farm on the left is the site of a Roman villa discovered in 1946; ahead lie the rather ordinary buildings in the village core; and to the right are the Old Barn Inn, the rectory and the small and unremarkable church.

If the difficulties involved in following the Gartree Road south-east from Glooston can be surmounted (either by using a car or by following footpaths and lanes through Slawston) it is worth visiting Medbourne, where substantial remains of the Roman period, including a large villa, have been discovered. In all probability there was a minor Roman settlement here. More recent artefacts include a four-arched medieval packhorse bridge, immediately west of the church, and the Nevill Arms, an excellent stone-built village pub with a fine range of food and real ale.

Notes

Maps OS 1:50,000 sheets 140 and 141.
Further reading W. G. Hoskins, *Leicestershire: A Shell Guide* (Faber & Faber, 1970); Nikolaus Pevsner, *The Buildings of England: Leicestershire and Rutland* (Penguin, 1960).
Public transport Frequent Leicester City Transport buses run between Leicester rail station and Stoughton Road, Stoneygate. In contrast Glooston is poorly served by public transport, though there is a morning bus (Tuesdays only) from Leicester to Market Harborough via Glooston, returning in early afternoon.

23

SEWSTERN LANE

Long Bennington to Sewstern 13 miles/21km

This is a quiet walk in remote countryside in the English Shires, following an ancient road once known as the Drift (a reference to its importance as a drove route) and in continuous and varied use for many centuries. Recently much of Sewstern Lane has been incorporated in the Viking Way long-distance path, bringing yet another class of traveller on to the route. For much of its course it is now a deserted green lane, a classic of its type.

Historical Background

Since the valleys were then impassable, the initial purpose of Sewstern Lane, as a link across the dry uplands of eastern Leicestershire between the Welland and Trent valleys, indicates its prehistoric origins. It passes close to the village of Harston, where Iron Age relics have been discovered, and was certainly in use then, and it may indeed have been in use even earlier, during the Bronze Age.

The Romans annexed the first few miles of the road at its southern end, from Stamford as far north as Stretton, as part of Ermine Street, but their trunk road then followed a more easterly alignment, and the remainder of Sewstern Lane was less intensively used. The Romans did not, however, entirely abandon the old road since it led to the villa site at Thistleton and, further on, to Roman iron workings at Brewer's Grave near Woolsthorpe.

During the Dark Ages the Roman Ermine Street was abandoned and the evidence seems to suggest that Sewstern Lane became once again a major through route. The village of Buckminster, as the placename indicates, was the site of an early monastery (possibly dating from the earliest Anglian invasions, in the seventh century) and a few miles to the north King Lud's Entrenchments, mysterious earthworks close to the old road, also appear to date from the Anglo-Saxon period. For miles the road forms the boundary of Leicestershire and Lincolnshire, a further indication of its antiquity and of its importance in the Dark Ages, when boundaries were first precisely established.

Travellers passing between the great medieval fairs at Nottingham and Stamford may have provided a good deal of Sewstern Lane's traffic in the early medieval period, though in the thirteenth century a more direct route was made, leaving the old road at Sproxton Thorns and running north to Nottingham via Waltham. This was the first of two circumstances which led to a reduced status for Sewstern Lane; the second was the lack of accommodation on the ancient route, which avoids villages for 27 miles between Stamford and Long Bennington. As a result most travellers chose to use the main coach route through Grantham, although the Earls of Rutland still used Sewstern Lane on their way from Belvoir Castle to London.

Cattle, too, continued to be driven along the road, giving it its new name of the Drift in the eighteenth century, as they were moved from the east Midlands to markets at Barnet, London and Maidstone. Finally, the construction of railways diverted the drovers and left Sewstern Lane abandoned, a superb example of a wide green lane.

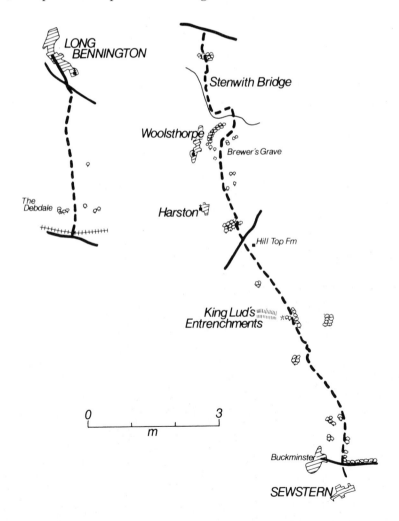

Description of the Route

Long Bennington is an unattractive commuter village, and the route of Sewstern Lane has to cross the A1 (Great North Road) on a modern bridge (SK840433), but after this unpromising start there is a rapid improvement, although for the first mile or so solitude is the chief virtue as the track traverses a low plateau. West of Allington it is joined by the Viking Way, a locally developed long-distance footpath from the Humber estuary to Oakham. Near Cox's Walk there is a level crossing over the Nottingham to Grantham railway line, and a little later the more formidable obstacle of the juggernaut-infested A52 has to be faced.

The farm lane south of the A52 is not particularly notable, but by the time the way approaches Stenwith Bridge it has become an excellent wide, green drove road, fringed by mature trees to the east. This character persists across a minor road, where there is a memorial stile provided by the Ramblers Association, as far as the trackbed of the former Belvoir Branch ironstone railway, opened in 1883 to export iron ore from near Brewer's Grave.

Across the trackbed the way lies through brambles for a few yards and then into a long, narrow enclosure running for ½ mile between the railway and

Sewstern Lane and the Ramblers Association memorial stile at Stenwith Bridge

The disused Grantham canal at Woolsthorpe Bridge. To the right of the canal is the wide green enclosure containing Sewstern Lane and the embankment of the former Belvoir ironstone railway

The church and Dysart mausoleum at Buckminster

the Grantham Canal. Clearly Sewstern Lane was of sufficient importance, even as late as 1883, for this strip of land to be preserved, flanked on either side by more modern forms of transport. The Grantham Canal, opened in 1797 and running for 33 miles between Grantham and Nottingham, was only truly profitable (carrying agricultural produce from Lincolnshire and coal, lime and building materials from Nottingham) before the Nottingham to Grantham railway opened in 1851. Nevertheless the canal company persevered, carrying iron ore from Brewer's Grave until that trade too fell to the railway, and the canal was abandoned only in 1936.

Sewstern Lane continues as a narrow path in a wide enclosure as far as Woolsthorpe Bridge, where the brick canal bridge, between two dilapidated locks, gives access to the Rutland Arms, a former bargee's pub now known as the Dirty Duck. The wide enclosure continues south of the bridge, but with no public access; instead, go through the dismantled railway bridge and either take a narrow footpath on the right, at the base of the railway embankment, or keep to a track going east to meet Longmoor Lane, and then turn right to rejoin the canal.

The two routes meet at another canal bridge. Cross both this and the former railway line and begin to climb, with a pleasant wooded valley on the left, to a plateau where Sewstern Lane exists as a cart-track with wide views left over arable land and right to Belvoir Castle. Ahead is a minor road and a Belvoir lodge on the site of Brewer's Grave, supposedly the last resting place of a Belvoir Castle brewer who drowned in a vat of his own ale.

After a slightly muddy start Sewstern Lane resumes its curving course as an enclosed cart-track running between large fields backed by mature woodland. After a mile another minor road is crossed. To the right lies Harston, where Iron Age remains were discovered in the 1930s in a quarry. The lane keeps straight on, now as the county boundary, which follows it almost as far as Sewstern, and crosses the A607 near Hill Top Farm. It is only ½ mile from here to Three Queens, now just a name on the map next to a mixed coniferous and elm plantation, but once an isolated inn specifically catering for travellers on the old road. Southwards from here the lane, still a wide green cattle drift enclosed by thick hedges, is a delight to walk. It approaches the Saltby to Wyville road through a clump of blackthorns, finds the modern road in occupation of the old line for a few yards, then plunges back into obscurity through a narrow gap where bushes have invaded the drift, before resuming as a track.

Over on the right, on the fringe of a forestry plantation, is the Tent, a tumulus reputed to be the burial place of King Lud (possibly the Mercian king, Ludeca, killed in battle in AD 827), and a little further away are King Lud's Entrenchments, Dark Age ditches of uncertain purpose. Next, the route

149

passes across the disused airfield on Saltby Heath, with the remains of various wartime buildings and one or two slight diversions away from the original direct route.

Saltby, where the prominent ironstone church stands away from the rest of the village, and Sproxton, notable for its wide village green, are too far away to warrant a detour, as is Coston, where Street Lane is yet another drovers' road, joining Sewstern Lane at Blue Point, south of Sewstern.

Sewstern Lane curves gradually to the right, is joined by the lane from Skillington, and approaches a slender-stalked water-tower partially hidden by a cocoon of trees. The lane at this point is a very wide dirt track, but after the tower it becomes, for the first time in miles, a metalled road, albeit only a narrow lane in the middle of the wide green strip. Before going on, however, it is worth travelling ½ mile west to Buckminster.

The early monastery at Buckminster has vanished without trace, but the church of St John Baptist, of light grey oolitic limestone, is especially attractive. Much of the church dates from the late thirteenth century, although the broach-spire is later. The unusual octagonal stone staircase in the nave, leading to the rood-loft and tower, is also worth examination. The effect of the church, gleaming white amongst the surrounding trees, is rather spoilt by the gloomy Victorian Gothic mausoleum in the churchyard. The village itself is a large and pleasant 'estate' village – Buckminster Hall, now largely demolished, was the seat of the Earls of Dysart.

There are views of Buckminster from the metalled Sewstern Lane, which continues straight ahead at a crossroads, now ominously signposted to 'Sewstern Industrial Estate'. The only evidence of this, however, is a widening of the road, which quickly reaches Sewstern post office and the end of the walk (SK892218). Most of the village, which is small and scattered, lies to the right – including the neo-Norman church of 1842 and the Blue Dog public house. The Viking Way continues south from Sewstern to Oakham – a tempting alternative to the bus?

Notes

Map   OS 1:50,000 sheet 130.
Further reading   W. G. Hoskins, *The Heritage of Leicestershire* (City of Leicester Publicity Department, 1950); Lincolnshire County Council, *The Viking Way* (County Council, 1983).
Public transport   Long Bennington has an adequate bus service to Grantham; alternatively, Bottesford station is on the Nottingham to Grantham line, and Sewstern Lane can be reached near the Debdale in 3 miles. Sewstern has infrequent buses to Grantham.

24

HIGH DIKE

Byard's Leap to Harmston Heath 8 miles/13km

The section of High Dike north of Byard's Leap, near Ancaster, towards Lincoln is one of the few stretches of Ermine Street, the vitally important Roman road north from London, not now followed by main roads. It forms a gentle, pleasant walk along tracks and minor roads, enlivened by views west towards the Trent valley and east over Lincoln Heath.

Historical Background

Lincoln Heath, part of the limestone ridge running north to south along the spine of the county, has seen long-distance travellers since the earliest times. The so-called 'Jurassic ridgeway' used the dry western scarp of the limestone uplands on its way from south-west England into Yorkshire and the north, and another prehistoric route, Mareham Lane, passed along the eastern edge of the limestone outcrop (which at times formed the coastline) between Bourne and the Lincoln Gap.

Lincolnshire was 'Romanised' very quickly after the invasion, with the major local tribe, the Coritani, offering little resistance to the Romans and becoming a 'client kingdom'. The invading army followed the existing lines of communication – the ridgeway and Mareham Lane – and later adapted and improved them, so that the ridgeway became part of Ermine Street and Mareham Lane the rather less important King Street.

Ermine Street, connecting London with Godmanchester, Lincoln and northern England, may originally have been planned as a frontier road, but this function was quickly usurped by the Fosse Way and thus Lincoln Heath was removed from the military zone, becoming instead an agricultural backwater administered from Ratae Coritanorum (Leicester). There are signs that the land was intensively farmed – for example, a number of corn-drying kilns have been discovered in the vicinity.

With the decline of the Roman Empire roads such as Ermine Street soon fell into disuse as through routes, and by the time the need for long-distance communications was re-established the focus of settlement had shifted and the natural line for such routes now lay below the limestone scarp. Gough's map, dating from the fourteenth century, indicates this transition: the Great

151

North Road from Stamford to Grantham and Newark is prominent, but no road is shown across Lincoln Heath.

The road from Lincoln to Sleaford and Bourne is shown on Ogilby's road atlas, published in 1675, and this road, roughly following Mareham Lane (the later King Street) was turnpiked in the eighteenth century. Not so Ermine Street (this section by now known as High Dike) between Ancaster and Lincoln. This section of the Roman trunk road became a green lane, used at times by drovers but otherwise only for local journeys. Now consisting of cart-tracks alternating with short lengths of country lane, it is the only substantial part of Ermine Street which can be walked in comfort.

Description of the Route

Start the walk to the north of Byard's Leap Farm (SK989499), where the B6403, which has been following the course of Ermine Street north from Ancaster (the Roman Cavsennae), reaches the A17 trunk road. The Roman legacy is easily seen, for the track is clearly situated upon the embankment of the Roman road, which at this point is some 40ft wide and is raised about three or four feet above its surroundings. But a more modern component of the landscape, the formless and extensive sprawl of RAF Cranwell, is unfortunately more likely to catch the eye.

Fortunately Ermine Street – or High Dike, as it is here known – quickly frees itself of this unwelcome neighbour and becomes a rural cart-track

High Dike on Leadenham Heath

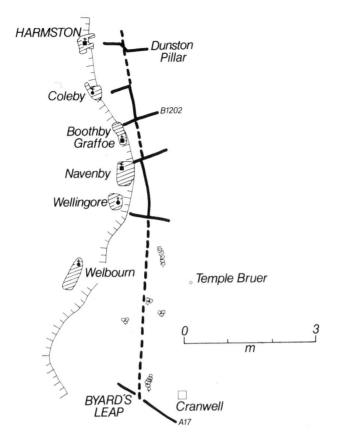

located within a very wide drove road. The Roman agger is now less clear and lower, having subsided over the centuries on to the surrounding land. A good deal of recent tree-planting has taken place on both sides of the Leadenham road junction, and it is to be hoped that the saplings survive the vandals, for High Dike is here well away from the western scarp of Lincoln Heath, and it traverses fairly undistinguished countryside for a mile or so.

Relief is not far away, however. The track reaches Cocked Hat Plantation and passes to the left of what remains of this previously attractive triangular piece of woodland, which has recently been butchered; a short stroll to the right leads to the remains of Temple Bruer, a preceptory of the Knights Templar founded in the reign of Henry II. There is a solid Early English tower, rising startlingly for some 50ft out of a farmyard; once this was connected by a cloister to a round church, a rarity in England, but there are few traces of this. The present diminutive Temple Bruer church, dating from 1874 and another mile across the fields, is not worth the extra walk.

Back on High Dike, now represented by a wide green lane north of Cocked Hat Plantation, the derelict structures of a wartime airfield can still be distinguished to the left. South of Griffin's Covert a narrow metalled lane comes in from the right and for the next 1½ miles this keeps to the line of the

153

Chapel at Wellingore.

Roman road. Fortunately it is not a through road and the low level of use to which it is subjected is reflected in the luxuriant growth of grass in the centre of the tarmac strip.

At a crossroads High Dike continues ahead as a country lane signposted to Navenby. After a while a footpath bears off left to Wellingore, an attractive stone-built village above the scarp, with a long, pedimented eighteenth-century hall, attached to which is a quasi-Romanesque Catholic chapel with a circular tower. A mile further north, via High Dike or the A607, is Navenby, a distinctly large village with a church whose tower collapsed in the eighteenth century and has since been rebuilt. There are several shops, although the antique and video shops outnumber the grocery concerns.

To the east of Navenby the course of High Dike is still represented by a minor road, now suburbanised as it passes rows of council houses; there is even a 'High Dyke' nameplate at one point. Northwards, however, it reverts to a green drift with the ruts of a cart-track disfiguring its central portion. Away to the west, again perched above the scarp slopes, is Boothby Graffoe, where the original church was 'extirpated by a hurricane' in 1666. The present church is Gothic Victorian, and the views across the wide Trent

Harmston church

valley to the west are rather more notable. Well to the west are the moats, earthworks and ruins of Somerton Castle, where King John of France was imprisoned after his capture at Poitiers in 1356.

North of the B1202 High Dike has the form of an extremely minor country road, heading north past a windpump to Coleby Heath. Coleby – above the scarp face to the west of the Roman road – is of no great interest, and a more interesting site lies away in the distance to the east. This is Dunston Pillar, which was built as a lighthouse (yes, this far inland!) in 1751. The intention was to guide travellers across the desolate, featureless Lincoln Heath. The light was replaced in 1810 by a statue of George III, and this too was removed in 1939 since it was considered to be a danger to aircraft. Now the pillar resembles nothing more romantic than a chimney-stack.

A rather attractive green lane takes up the line of the Roman road from Coleby Heath towards Lincoln. On the approach to Harmston Heath the lane, now a reddish-brown track, is confined between hedgerows and tall trees. The ground rises slowly and then the track merges with a lay-by formed from a complex junction with the B1178 (SK986622). Ahead are the prominent buildings of Waddington airfield, and the ignominious end of High Dike as a cul-de-sac robbed of its approach to Lincoln by the encroachment of the airfield.

The OS map indicates the precision with which the Roman road is followed, first by the parish boundary and then by minor roads east of the overspill village of Waddington; then, after a gap, the A607 takes up the alignment for a short distance. Another parish boundary, not followed by a right of way, takes High Dike into Lincoln itself.

Sadly it is not possible to walk into Lincoln by the route just described. So turn left along the B1178, cross the A607 and explore Harmston, its eighteenth-century hall now a hospital and its church of All Saints possessing an immediately post-Conquest Norman tower but little else dating back before a thorough restoration in 1868. A cliff-edge village, Harmston has an attractive mixture of cottages and a cosy intimacy derived from its close-knit pattern of streets and back lanes. Lincoln – and Ermine Street, for that matter – seems a long way away.

Notes

Maps   OS 1;50,000 sheet 121 (and, for the first ¼ mile, sheet 130).
Further reading   Walter Marsden, *Lincolnshire* (Batsford, 1977); Jack Yates and Henry Thorold, *Lincolnshire: A Shell Guide* (Faber & Faber, 1965).
Public transport   There is an hourly bus service from Lincoln south-wards, calling at both Harmston and Leadenham (west of Byard's Leap).

25

THE OLD PORTWAY

Wirksworth to Ashford in the Water 13 miles/21km

The walk follows a succession of minor lanes, bridleways and footpaths which between them preserve the course of a Saxon through route (itself an adaptation of a prehistoric ridgeway) across the White Peak limestone plateau in Derbyshire.

Historical Background

The name of the Old Portway dates from Saxon times, but as a thoroughfare it can be traced a great deal further than that – indeed, it is widely regarded as the most ancient road in Derbyshire. Its prehistoric origins stem from its qualities as an obvious ridgeway, avoiding valleys wherever possible as it crosses the limestone country known as the White Peak. This may have been one of the routes by which the stone axes manufactured in the Lake District were distributed to southern England. Certainly it fulfilled more local transport needs, linking the Iron Age hill-forts of Mam Tor, Fin Cop and Castle Ring, and also passing close to the burial mounds on Stanton Moor and at Harboro Rocks, and to the stone circles on Harthill Moor.

The Romans undoubtedly knew of the trackway – lead was mined at Wirksworth in Roman times – and they may have used parts of it, but the next undisputed travellers along the trackway were the Saxons. A string of 'portway' placenames emphasises the point: the 'Porthway' at Griffe Grange, Portaway lead mines near Winster, the village of Alport, and reference to the Portway in a Bakewell charter.

The Old Portway continued in use in medieval times, when the portion from Bakewell northwards acquired the alternative name of Castlegate, and other parts of the route became known variously as Islington Lane (taking its name from a now deserted village near Winster), Dark Lane and even the Chariot Way. The growth of the lead-mining industry in the area north of Wirksworth led to renewed use of the route, and the eighteenth century also saw packhorse trains plodding along the Old Portway, until the railways and turnpike roads combined to draw trade away from the ancient trackway for the final time.

Description of the Route

Wirksworth, largely ignored by the tourists and presenting a rather unprepossessing face to the world, nevertheless has a remarkable and varied past. A focal point for five ancient tracks, including the prehistoric Old Portway and the track which the Romans transformed into Hereward Street, it later became a centre of the lead-mining industry and has since seen its surrounding hills devastated by limestone quarrying.

More attractive reminders of its former prosperity are the imposing 'lead church' in its circular churchyard (a sure sign of an early foundation, and indeed there has been a church here since the seventh century) and the town houses huddled along the main streets as they climb towards the Market Place. The Moot Hall, meeting place of the lead-miners' Barmote Court, is a reconstruction of 1814 and is of little aesthetic value; inside is the fourteen-pint brass measuring dish given by Henry VIII in 1513.

The Old Portway entered Wirksworth from the south, coming from the significantly named Alport Height. Direct progress northwards from the town is ruled out, however, by the steep-sided dry valleys around Middleton and the need to cross the deeply incised lower section of the Griffe Grange valley, and so the route turns west to begin with. Take the B5035, then turn right on to the lane past Norbreck Farm to Gallows Knoll and the bridleway leading north (from SK252546) across the former monastic holding of Griffe Grange. Settled by the Scandinavians in the tenth century – 'gryfja' is Old Norse for 'deep, narrow valley' – Griffe Grange became a sheep farm belonging to Darley Abbey in the twelfth century.

To the west here lies the Upper Golconda mine, with its 3 miles of underground galleries, and further west are Harboro Rocks, site of a neolithic chambered tomb and of a cave which was inhabited from the neolithic period until the eighteenth century. But the Old Portway, also known in this section as the Chariot Way, continues north-west as a broad green lane between white limestone walls as far as the hamlet of Grangemill. Both Grangemill and Aldwark, a mile to the west, were monastic settlements. The disused mill at Grangemill was supplied with water from a pond (which still exists) formed on a bed of volcanic lava in the middle of the limestone plateau.

Between Grangemill and the outskirts of Winster there is little alternative to the B5056, which represents the course of the Old Portway for about 1½ miles. To the right is Wyns Tor, one of a series of limestone tors dominating Winster. Bear left, then go straight across a minor road some 200 yards before the Miner's Standard, an excellent pub with a name which emphasises the former dependence on lead-mining of Winster – a village which grew

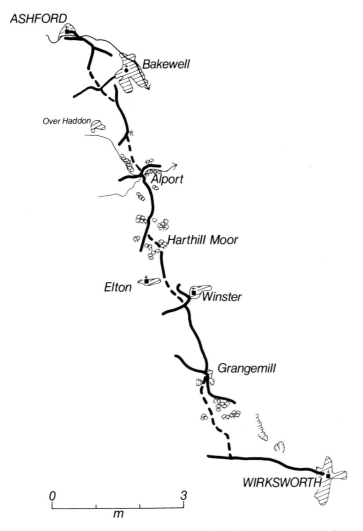

ASHFORD

Bakewell

Over Haddon

Alport

Harthill Moor

Elton

Winster

Grangemill

WIRKSWORTH

0 _____ 3
m

quickly to market-town status at the end of the seventeenth century. Now there is just an empty market place, a series of narrow alleys, and some fine Georgian town houses near the market hall, its ground floor arches originally open but now filled in.

The lane by-passing Winster to the west is called Islington Lane, a reference to the former village of Islington, which has vanished from the landscape but probably lay to the north-east of Westhill Farm. This is an excellent green lane crossing a shallow dry valley to the Elton road, beyond which it drops quite steeply past the disused seventeenth-century Portaway lead mine to a junction with the B5056. But the route of the Old Portway is here taken up by a track which ascends close to the edge of a wood, with the old paving quite clearly visible, and then suddenly emerges on to Harthill Moor, an area of quite extraordinary interest.

159

The paved section of the Old Portway on the climb towards Robin Hood's Stride

To the right are Cratcliff Rocks, housing a hermit's cave with, hewn from the bare rock, a seat, a crucifix and a recess which housed a lamp. To the left the striking outcrop is known as Robin Hood's Stride, named after the twin rock tors some 20 yards apart. In front, and just to the right of the path, is a large oval earthwork which may have protected an Iron Age settlement. Further north is a standing stone and the scanty remains of a Bronze Age stone circle of which only four stones remain. And through the centre of Harthill Moor runs the Old Portway, its course generally tracing a slight hollow across the moor.

The path continues north-west to a minor road; straight across here is a lane leading to Harthill Moor Farm, in whose backyard lies the bank and ditch of Castle Ring, a small Iron Age hill-fort overlooking the River Bradford and Lathkill Dale. But the way lies north, along the minor road to Alport, a pleasant hamlet hugging the valley bottom at the confluence of the Lathkill and Bradford.

Alport's name betrays its links with the Old Portway, which crossed the Lathkill here by means of an ancient ford, and its former importance as a market centre. There are some fine seventeenth-century houses, especially the gabled Monks Hall, together with the remains of a smelt mill serving the nearby lead mines. At the height of its industrial prosperity there were two cupolas in the valley bottom, with condensing flues climbing the steep hillside to a tall chimney which made use of the high winds whistling around the limestone plateau. Now only the chimney and the derelict flues remain.

The Old Portway climbed steeply out of the Lathkill gorge via Dark Lane, a narrow track quite correctly signposted as unfit for motor vehicles, which reaches the plateau close to one of the many fluorspar mines in the district. Fluorspar, which is used as a flux in open-hearth steel-making, has only been worked commercially in the White Peak for about eighty years, but now more than 200,000 tons a year are mined in the area between Castleton and Wirksworth.

Dark Lane peters out into a bridleway enclosed to the east by the boundary wall of Haddon Fields – a reminder that down in the Wye valley to the right is Haddon Hall, the mansion which Pevsner has described as 'the English castle *par excellence*'. The major rebuilding of the hall in 1350 spelt the end for the village of Nether Haddon, because the site was required for the

Sheepwash Bridge, Ashford-in-the-Water

enlarged park surrounding the hall; the village was larger than its twin, Over Haddon (½ a mile away on its ledge overlooking the densely wooded Lathkill Dale) in 1334 but had been completely depopulated by 1431.

The bridleway continues north towards a tumulus by an OS pillar; here it joins the Bakewell road, which is followed for ½ mile below Ditch Cliff, until a footpath on the left indicates the line of the Old Portway. Bakewell, an important Saxon settlement – there is a Saxon cross in the churchyard and Castle Hill was probably fortified before the Norman Conquest – lies less than a mile away, and with its impressive parish church, lively cattle market, Bakewell pudding shop and Old House museum, is worth a visit.

The Old Portway, which by now has also acquired the name of Castlegate since in medieval times it led to Ashford castle, takes the path below Ditch Cliff and Burton Moor to reach a minor crossroads. The lane straight across represents the course of the ancient track at first, but after this curves away to the right the true line is lost, and not even the field boundaries offer clues to its whereabouts. There is no alternative, therefore, to the lane which runs down to the A6 and, after a few hundred yards, Ashford in the Water (SK195697).

Ashford has suffered at the hands of both tourists and commuters, but for all that it is an attractive stone village with three bridges crossing the River Wye. Sheepwash Bridge, the oldest and most picturesque with its attached sheepfold, replaced the ford which carried the prehistoric track and Saxon portway across the River Wye. The church was extensively rebuilt in 1870, and the village's mills are more interesting. There is a corn mill at the eastern end of the village, and ½ mile to the west was a mill used in dressing the 'black marble' for which Ashford was renowned. First quarried in 1748, the marble was actually an impure limestone used in ornamental work, and examples survive in Chatsworth House and Ashford church.

Notes

Maps OS 1:25,000 Outdoor Leisure sheet 24 (The White Peak) or 1:50,000 sheet 119.

Further reading F. R. Banks, *The Peak District* (Robert Hale, 1975); A. E. and E. M. Dodd, *Peakland Roads and Trackways* (Moorland, 2nd edn. 1980); Roy Millward and Adrian Robinson, *The Peak District* (Eyre Methuen, 1975).

Public transport Wirksworth has hourly buses from Derby, Matlock and Bakewell, while Ashford is served by the Buxton to Bakewell service (six buses a day on weekdays, plus a summer Sunday service).

26

PACKHORSE WAYS
IN THE PEAK DISTRICT

Hayfield to Castleton 9 miles/14km
with notes on routes back to Hayfield (a further 10 miles/16km)

The Dark Peak east of Glossop and Chapel-en-le-Frith is riddled with packhorse routes, many of them using older tracks and some of them used at the same time as corpse roads or saltways. This walk traces the course of one of the most important, skirting the fringe of the Kinder Scout massif on its way from Hayfield to the Vale of Edale and the Norman new town of Castleton.

Historical Background

The packhorse ways of the Dark Peak are a prominent and familiar part of the landscape of the area, whether they survive as walled green lanes, roughly paved tracks across marshy moorland or rutted holloways on firmer ground. The packhorse owners – one family of whom later began the Pickfords removal firm – were locally known as jaggers, and there are several Jaggers Lanes indicating the routes which they followed. The packhorse trails were important as through trade routes in the later medieval period, with salt from Cheshire, malt and wood from Derby, and lead, wool and charcoal amongst the most frequent loads for the pack trains. The construction of the turnpike roads from the late eighteenth century onwards finally brought the end of the packhorse trade.

   The track from Hayfield over the flanks of the Kinder Scout plateau was an important early medieval route, and with the growth of the packhorse trade it became part of a vital link between the Manchester area and Derbyshire. Its former importance is indicated by the paved sections which still exist, and by the way in which parts of the route have become holloways as a result of the volume of traffic using the track.

   East of Grindsbrook Booth in the Vale of Edale the main route continued to Edale End and Hope, but another way climbed south to Hollins Cross and then descended the hill slopes to Castleton. This was also the corpse road

163

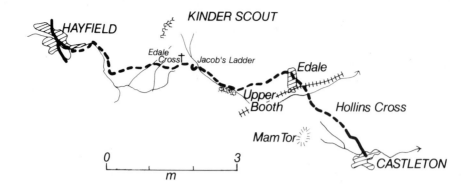

over which the dead were carried for burial in Castleton before Edale church was consecrated in the seventeenth century. Later still, Castleton women used the track on their journey to work at the mill in Edale.

The multiple use of the ancient ways is illustrated by the two old routes west from the Castleton area. The ridge route from Hollins Cross to the Mam Tor hill-fort and Rushup Edge was a prehistoric ridgeway, later used by packhorses, and the road through the Winnats Pass, once a packhorse route, was also a saltway used in carrying the salt from Cheshire to Sheffield and south Yorkshire.

Description of the Route

Hayfield, hemmed in nowadays by industry to the west and the moors of the Dark Peak to the east, was an important gathering point for the packhorse trains of the late medieval period. Packways led south, over Mount Famine to Rushup Edge and Tideswell; south-east, past Edale Cross into the Vale of Edale; and north, through Glossop to Holmfirth, where wool carried by the packhorses from the Hayfield mills was dyed. Now Hayfield is dominated by its industry, including textile manufacturing, paper-making and calico-printing, and there is little else of note. Even the church, close to the River Sett, dates only from 1818, its predecessor having been swept away in floods.

The walk begins at the Royal Hotel in Hayfield (SK037870). Take the road forcing its way up the steep-sided Sett valley towards Kinder reservoir; leave the road shortly after passing a car park and climb past Hill House Farm (fork right here) and west of Tunstead Clough Farm on a clearly marked track running south. At Coldwell Clough the packhorse track changes direction abruptly to the east and begins to climb steadily as a holloway, occasionally dropping down into minor valleys (the crossing of Oaken Clough Brook is marked on the map as Stony Ford) to reach Edale Cross at 1,750ft (533m) on the col between Kinder Low and Brown Knoll.

The Hambleton Drove Road on the northern slopes of Black Hamilton

164

Edale Cross is almost certainly early medieval, although it appears to be dated 1610 and after having collapsed was re-erected in 1810 by local farmers (one of whom, John Gee, carved his initials on it). Its original purpose may have been to mark the boundary of the lands owned by Basingwerk Abbey in Flintshire, but it has been used by pilgrims, traders and more recently ramblers as a much-needed landmark in the largely featureless Kinder moorland.

East of Edale Cross the way descends, gradually at first, along the bad-weather alternative route of the Pennine Way into Edale Head, a vast amphitheatre hemmed in by crags in its upper reaches. Suddenly the path, sections of which are roughly paved, steepens at the top of Jacob's Ladder. The 'ladder' was the work of Jacob Marshall, who hacked out a short-cut in the eighteenth century, but now the steep slope is so badly eroded that the 'official' route avoids it by dropping into the valley on the left. It is much preferable, however, to follow the more circuitous zigzag route to the right (followed by the packhorses, who were unable to negotiate the direct route) which leads over paved slabs to the ruins of Edale Head House.

At the bottom of Jacob's Ladder the way crosses the infant River Noe by means of a substantial packhorse bridge. Now the route is particularly well defined past Lee House to Upper Booth, one of five vaccaries (cattle farms owned by the Crown) which occupied the sheltered south-facing slopes of the Vale of Edale in medieval times. All the others — Barber Booth, Grindsbrook Booth, Ollerbrook Booth and Nether Booth — were in being by the sixteenth century.

From Upper Booth take the path (still part of the Pennine Way) heading east to Grindsbrook Booth and the village of Edale, which these days is very much geared to meeting the needs of Pennine wayfarers and other, more vicarious, tourists: the Pennine Way, which starts here, was established in 1951. Yet until the coming of the railway in 1894 this was a remote backwater, a side-valley which concentrated on farming. There was, however, a corn mill established beside the River Noe in the seventeenth century; later it became a lace-thread spinning mill, then a tannery, and more recently it has been converted into flats.

Edale church, last rebuilt in 1885, was first consecrated in 1633. Until then, the packhorse way over Hollins Cross to Castleton also served as a corpse road. The way starts from the valley road west of Skinners Hall and climbs past Hollins Farm to the ridge between Mam Tor, the 'shivering mountain' topped by an Iron Age hill-fort, and Lose Hill at Hollins Cross.

The Roman road on the summit plateau of High Street, looking north to the Straits of Riggindale

Edale Cross, at the highest point on the packhorse route from Hayfield to Edale

There is a fine view north from here over the Vale of Edale to the desolate Kinder Scout plateau. The cross is recent, in memory of a local walker.

Now the path abruptly descends into Hope Vale, with Castleton conspicuous in the middle distance. The path, in some places paved in a rather rudimentary fashion, becomes enclosed and takes on the name of Hollowford Road. For some time the way lies down a deep holloway, then as the gradient eases the road becomes surfaced and a stream joins in from the right. This stream was presumably crossed by a ford in the hollow just north of Castleton; the 'hollowford' appears in documents in 1455.

The lane reaches the main road through Castleton at a sharp bend (SK151829); the centre of this tourist trap of a village lies to the right. A new town of the Norman era, Castleton was protected by a town ditch (of which there are some signs east of the centre) and a castle magnificently sited on the

The ruins of Edale Head House and the descent to the Noe valley near Jacob's Ladder (the white scar in the middle distance)

limestone cliff overlooking the town. Peveril Castle, built in the eleventh century by William Peveril and greatly extended in 1176 by Henry II, became a hunting lodge conveniently situated for the Royal Forest of the Peak, but was later neglected. The town suffered a similar fate; by late medieval times there were no markets, and Castleton never expanded to fill the area enclosed by the original town ditch.

Now, however, the tourists who come to see the castle or the limestone caverns – Blue John, Speedwell, Treak Cliff and Peak Caverns, the last of these described as 'a marvel of England' as early as the twelfth century – have been responsible for a considerable revival. Sadly, however, the traffic jams and gift shops tend to obscure the more attractive qualities of the place, such as the narrow streets around the church and the former market place, with Peveril Castle dominating the views south.

Ancient Routes Back to Hayfield

A long circular walk (possibly spread over two days) can be devised using ancient trackways to Rushup Edge and Hayfield. From Castleton there is a choice of two routes: by road through the Winnats Pass, a spectacular cleft which was followed by a medieval saltway and then a turnpike road, but which is now sadly traffic-ridden following the collapse of the former main road below Mam Tor; or, pleasanter but longer, back to Hollins Cross and then along the prehistoric ridgeway (also tackled later by the packhorses) across the summit plateau of Mam Tor.

The two routes meet at the col west of Mam Tor, then take the ridge west to Lord's Seat, where there is a Bronze Age burial mound, and Rushup Edge. The ridge route now meets the A625, but after only a hundred yards a bridleway leads north-west. This is yet another packhorse route, this time leading from Tideswell to Hayfield. The lane runs in places between high walls as it crosses Roych Clough and negotiates Mount Famine at about 1,400ft, finally descending into Hayfield along a narrow track hollowed out by the passage of time and countless packhorse trains.

Notes

Maps   OS 1:25,000 Outdoor Leisure sheet 1 (The Dark Peak) or 1:50,000 sheet 110.

Further reading   A. E. and E. M. Dodd, *Peakland Roads and Trackways* (Moorland, 2nd edn. 1980); Shirley Toulson, *Derbyshire: Exploring the Ancient Tracks and Mysteries of Mercia* (Wildwood House, 1980).

Public transport   Hayfield has an hourly service seven days a week to Stockport and a service to New Mills with a rail connection to Manchester. Castleton has a direct bus service from Sheffield (nine buses a day, including Sundays) and summer Sunday services from Manchester and Buxton.

27

WADE'S CAUSEWAY

Cawthorne to Grosmont 11 miles/18km

Part of the Roman road from Amotherby, near Malton, to Whitby is known as Wade's Causeway. The first few miles across the Vale of Pickering are difficult to follow, and the last few miles north of Grosmont are uncertain, but the central section across the bleak plateau of the North York Moors is superb, and on Wheeldale Moor a ¾ mile length of the 'causeway' has been exposed and is now in the care of the Department of the Environment – a magnificent and highly unusual ancient monument.

Historical Background

Wade's Causeway is the name given to the Roman road which ran between Amotherby, to the west of Malton (continuing the line of a road from York), and the north Yorkshire coast in the vicinity of Whitby. It was probably built in about AD 80, although there is the possibility that construction was actually completed somewhat later (an inscribed stone found near Julian

Looking north along Wade's Causeway towards the valley of the Wheeldale Gill

Park supports this theory). It seems to have been in use for a particularly short period – perhaps as little as four or five decades – possibly because its location was peripheral, its course across the bleak moors exposed and its purpose never really clear even to the Romans themselves.

One specific role for the highway appears to have been the transportation of Whitby jet, the most prized of the local minerals, from its source to York, where it was made up into ornaments (as indeed it had been in pre-Roman times). But the military use of the road was negligible, and it soon became derelict. Even when later roads followed the same general direction they did not often re-use the Roman route, which commonly lies close to but is ignored by modern minor roads.

Over the centuries the road surface became overgrown and eventually buried, and it was as late as the eighteenth century that its course was rediscovered by a local historian. It was again uncovered by a gamekeeper, James Patterson, in the 1890s, and finally the Office of Works exposed about a mile of it on Wheeldale Moor in 1912–15. It is now carefully preserved and maintained as an ancient monument (though it should be said that it does not represent a true picture of a Roman road, but merely an illustration of the foundation layers exposed by the erosion of the original surface).

Description of the Route

The Roman road appears to have approached Cawthorne from the south along what is now the notably straight narrow lane from Wrelton, passing through West Cawthorne farmyard and then turning north-east. Cawthorne (SE775891), a tiny hamlet these days, was once much larger and the fields around the two remaining farms contain evidence of the former site of a village. A barn in the hamlet is, according to Harry Mead, known as Bibo House – 'the Roman term for an inn . . . it could be that the Roman legionnaires refreshed themselves at this spot after tramping across the moors on Wade's Causeway'.

There is no obvious sign of the Roman road from the top of Cawthorne Lane, and no practical way of following its exact course for a while. This is particularly unfortunate since there are Roman practice works marked on the map only ½ mile away. The earthworks, which seem to consist of four camps covering several acres, were probably constructed as part of manoeuvres rather than to secure the safety of travellers along the road. Overgrown by scrub and partly hidden by forestry plantations, they can nevertheless be picked out from the lane running north to Keldy Banks.

A bridleway leads on from here, on the approximate line of the road, above the steep escarpment to Elleron Lodge and, via Middle Head Road (which is

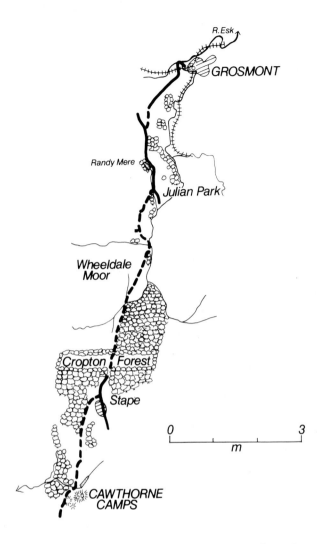

somewhat to the west of the true line) past the hamlet of Stape. On the left during this section is the extensive Cropton Forest, planted in the early 1920s and containing Keldy Castle, where the Victorian Gothic extravagance has been demolished. This is one of the areas where the Forestry Commission has made notable attempts to encourage recreation within its forests, and there are waymarked walks, nature trails and an outdoor pursuits centre. Nevertheless, until sixty years ago this was open moorland: now more than 30,000 acres in this sector of the North York Moors are afforested.

To the north of Stape Farm the present valley road probably indicates the Roman route past the waterfall near Hill Top Farm; then it lies to the east of the present road from Old Wives' Well, where the agger is just traceable, to Mauley Cross, near the highest point of the walk at 820ft (250m). The cross is

173

Wade's Causeway: sheep walk south along the exposed section of the Roman road on Wheeldale Moor

said to commemorate Peter de Mauley, who held the manors of Julian Park (visited later on this walk) and Mulgrave, the latter as a reward for blinding and later murdering Prince Arthur of Brittany, the only obstacle to Prince John's succession to the throne after Henry II and Richard Coeur de Lion.

The lane now runs northward through the forest to Keys Beck House, where the trees are replaced by heather moor to the left but still crowd in on the right. The Roman road lies in the trees all the way, its course still discernible for those prepared to face the physical and other consequences of rummaging about in the forest. The rewards are, in any case, very slight indeed compared with the section of exposed Roman road which lies on the other side of Wheeldale Bridge.

Just beyond the bridge Wade's Causeway departs at an acute angle from the moorland road, and for the next mile or so walkers can savour the superb experience of tramping on or alongside the longest exposed section of Roman road in Britain. What remains of the road itself, which is some 16ft wide, is essentially the large foundation stones, for the much finer surface layer of gravel has been eroded away. The culverts draining the road at intervals are an important reminder of the high standard of construction. On either side of the road itself are gullies worn down further by curious pedestrians since the road was first properly excavated by the Office of Works just before World War I. Now it is in the care of the Department of the Environment, although there is free access.

Although the road is unquestionably Roman in origin, it has become irrevocably associated with Wade, a Saxon chief of the eighth century who lived at Mulgrave. All manner of tall stories link the 'giant' Wade and his wife Bel with the causeway, perhaps the best of which suggests that they built it to connect their castles at Pickering and Mulgrave, Bel carrying the stones in her apron and the two of them using a hammer which they threw to each other – whilst standing 17 miles apart!

About half-way along the causeway a rutted track leads down to the right, into the deep valley of Wheeldale Beck and, via stepping stones over the beck, to the delightfully situated Wheeldale youth hostel. The way along the Roman road continues through a gate, the boulders seemingly becoming even bigger as the causeway begins to descend a comparatively steep slope. This is perhaps the most picturesque section, the big stones of the road leading the eye into and across the wooded valley of the Wheeldale Gill. At the next gate the Roman causeway abruptly disappears, but a footpath continues next to the right-hand field wall, over a stile and across a field to a footbridge which crosses the Wheeldale Gill in a little glade.

Wheeldale Youth Hostel

To the right is a concrete ford over the main stream, now called West Beck, but the way lies straight ahead, following the signposted but initially rather overgrown bridleway up to Hazel Head Farm and then north along a farm lane (almost certainly true to its Roman predecessor) past Hollin Head to Julian Park. This has been claimed as the site of a Roman villa, and an inscribed stone was discovered here with the inscrutable message 'Fifty standard-bearing soldiers of the Sixth Legion, the Victorious'. The legion was stationed in York early in the second century AD and could possibly have built the road. Moss Swang, a glacial overflow channel, runs north from near Julian Park towards the Esk valley.

At Julian Park the Roman route is now followed by the minor but quite well-used road which snakes round from Goathland to Egton Bridge. The road runs past the mysterious and not very conspicuous earthwork known as the Park Dike, and then skirts the interestingly named Randy Mere reservoir, previously hemmed in by conifers but now easily seen in its deep bowl following clear felling in 1984. Half a mile further on, before the cottage at Struntry Carr, the Roman road disappears into Combs Wood; from now on only its modern successors can be followed.

Beyond the wood take the second bridleway on the right, to join a lane west of High Burrows, and keep to this past Low Burrows – where the Romans established a minor camp, still faintly visible – and along Lease Rigg before descending steeply down to the Esk valley at Grosmont (NZ828053), once a vital source of iron ore for the growing ironworks in north-east England, and still bearing the legacy of its industrial past in disused quarries and tips of iron shale. The Roman road clearly crossed the River Esk at Grosmont, but its course thereafter is uncertain and this is as good a place as any to end the journey – though one final call could be made (by train if necessary) to Egton Bridge, famous for its annual Gooseberry Show.

Notes

Map OS 1:25,000 Outdoor Leisure sheet 27 (The North York Moors – East).

Further reading Malcolm Barker, *Yorkshire: the North Riding* (Batsford, 1977); Maurice Colbeck, *Yorkshire Moorlands* (Batsford, 1983); Harry Mead, *Inside the North York Moors* (David & Charles, 1978).

Public transport The nearest buses to Cawthorne run to Pickering, which has a frequent service from Scarborough. Grosmont is on the Middlesbrough to Whitby railway line, with a roughly two-hourly service. But the ideal way to tackle this walk is to take a steam train on the North York Moors Railway from Grosmont to Pickering and walk back via Cawthorne and Wheeldale Moor – a walk of about 15 miles (24km).

28

THE HAMBLETON DROVE ROAD

Sheep Wash to Sutton Bank 11 miles/18km

The Hambleton Drove Road is a classic ridge route traversing the length of the Hambleton Hills, with wide-ranging views over the Vale of York and into the North York Moors National Park. Part of an ancient trackway linking southern England with eastern Scotland, it became a vitally important drovers' road providing access to markets at Malton and York. Nowadays one section forms part of the route of the Cleveland Way long-distance path.

Historical Background

Hambleton Street, as it is often called, has a much longer pedigree than its fame as a drove road would suggest. The description 'street' hints at Roman origins, but the Romans made little use of the route, although there is a pottery kiln near Oldstead; prehistoric man, however, appears to have been a regular traveller along the road.

The evidence for prehistoric use of the Hambleton road lies mainly in the concentration of burial mounds, forts and cross-dykes along the line of the route. The New Stone Age is represented by a tumulus above Kepwick, the Bronze Age by the round barrows which lie close to the road, and the Iron Age by the promontory fort at Boltby and – perhaps, since their exact date is a matter for speculation – the cross-dykes and other earthworks south of High Paradise.

The Hambleton Road continued in use throughout the medieval period as part of a major through route between London and Scotland – the precursor of the Great North Road. It saw the passage of armies, monks from the five nearby monasteries, and Scots raiders on cattle-thieving incursions. William the Conqueror is reputed to have used it whilst crushing a northern rebellion in 1069, and Edward II certainly came this way in 1322, retreating southwards after the failure of his bid to invade Scotland. Scotch Corner, near Oldstead, marks the spot where Robert Bruce caught up with and routed the English army.

The dawn of the turnpike era saw a temporary decline in the importance of the Hambleton Road, which was never improved from its rough, unsurfaced condition and therefore could not be used by wheeled traffic. Instead the stage-coaches and wagons used the newer, lower road through the Vale of Mowbray.

The ridge route was by no means abandoned, however. Since turnpikes were expensive to use, cattle and sheep were still driven to market along the old green road. As droving reached its peak in the eighteenth century, the Hambleton Road became heavily used by Scottish drovers, to the extent that more than 25,000 cattle a year passed over Wetherby bridge after having negotiated the route along the Hambleton ridge. Many were Galloways or West Highlands (also known as Kyloes) on their way south from Falkirk Tryst to London's Smithfield market or the smaller markets at York or Malton.

The droves climbed up from the Cleveland plain through Scarth Nick to the northern slopes of Black Hambleton and continued south along the ridge (possibly resting overnight at the stance beside the old inn at Limekiln House) to Sutton Bank and Oldstead. Here the route divided, the left-hand branch crossing the Howardian Hills to Malton and the more popular right fork leading further south to York and London. Parts of the drovers' route now form minor country roads, but between Black Hambleton and Sneck Yate the ancient track across the heather moor is comparatively and enticingly unchanged.

Description of the Route

The best place to start the walk is at Sheep Wash (SE471994), about 1½ miles north-east of the large village of Osmotherley. The drove road comes in from the north as a metalled road, having climbed from the Cleveland plain by ascending Scarth Nick, a glacial overflow channel, and after fording Crabdale Beck it leaves to the south as High Lane, a roughly surfaced track running to the east of a forestry plantation. After about a mile the road from Osmotherley comes in from the right; in high summer and at weekends this junction is festooned with picnickers' cars.

Follow the road south past Chequers, now a farmhouse offering afternoon teas but once an inn of some renown – one of four (three of which are now closed) along the Hambleton stretch of the drove road. Cross Slapestones Beck, noting the fine views west over the Vale of Mowbray, and after five minutes or so keep on where the road swerves left at Oakdale Head, and begin to climb, accompanied now by the Cleveland Way long-distance footpath, the massive northern shoulder of Black Hambleton.

This first real climb, along a rutted track across heathery moorland, is none too difficult but should be taken slowly in order to appreciate the surroundings. Another blanket of Forestry Commission conifers wrecks any hopes of views to the west at first, but the wide and colourful moorland of Hambleton End in front combines with the long retrospective views along Hambleton Street to compel frequent halts. Later the path leaves the edge of the forest and, passing a tumulus, gains the extensive summit plateau of Black Hambleton.

Now the best part of the drove road is underfoot. The path is visible for miles as it crosses a grouse moor, losing height gradually as far as White Gill Head at the very edge of the escarpment. Down to the right are the spring-line villages of the Vale of Mowbray, while on the left there are glimpses of the North York Moors proper. At the side of the track, much of it now enclosed by stone walls, there are disused limestone quarries, and the remains of the second drovers' pub, significantly named Limekiln House, can be seen,

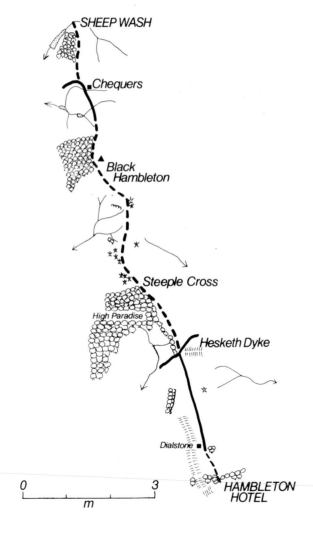

SHEEP WASH

Chequers

Black
Hambleton

Steeple Cross

High Paradise

Hesketh Dyke

Dialstone

HAMBLETON
HOTEL

0   3
    m

Chequers Farm, formerly an inn on the Hambleton drove road

although the passage of time has reduced the building and its adjacent cattle stance to a few heaps of rubble.

Less than a mile to the south is Steeple Cross, marking the junction of the drove road and the ancient green lane connecting Kepwick and Helmsley. Only the stump of the cross remains, and Friars Cross, which lay a little to the west, seems to have disappeared completely. The names of the crosses, and the fact that the drove road around here was once known as the Lord's Tongue, suggest a substantial monastic use of the ancient tracks in medieval times.

Southwards from Steeple Cross the drove road skirts another forest, traverses Dale Town Common, which is pockmarked with disused quarries, and reaches the lane leading to the quixotically named High Paradise Farm. Here the drovers' route parts company with the Cleveland Way, which passes the farm and then keeps close to the top of the scarp all the way to Sutton Bank. The drove road, however, steers a more easterly course, still as a wide green drift between gleaming white limestone walls. So wide is the space between the walls that there is room for the white and rutted High Paradise access road and a greener walkers' track, the two of them separated by a shallow ditch.

At the top of Sneck Yate Bank there is some welcome shade provided by tall trees; less welcome is the change in the character of Hambleton Street to a single-track metalled road, though it is furnished with very wide grass verges and in any case there is little motor traffic. Just to the east of Sneck Yate runs Hesketh Dike, of uncertain age and purpose.

The next stretch of the drove route is known as Cleveland Road, and it runs, for 2 miles, in a dead straight and rather uninteresting line to Dialstone Farm. (The Cleveland Way, following the scarp, is more interesting as it skirts the hill-fort on Boltby Scar and reaches Whitestone Cliff, from where Dialstone Farm can easily be reached.) The farm was once the third of the drovers' inns, although it also catered for the racing fraternity based at Hambleton House, and the dial stone, used for weighing jockeys, from which the inn was named can be seen in the wall opposite the farm.

Take the green lane pointing straight ahead at the crossroads south of Dialstone Farm. The lane leads to Hambleton House, still a racing stable but now the only reminder of the days when Hambleton Down racecourse was known as the 'Newmarket of the North'. Its heyday was in the seventeenth century; its inaccessibility gradually told against it, and in 1755 the most important race, the Queen Anne Plate, was transferred to York. The last meeting was held in 1811.

Just to the south of the stables is the Hambleton Hotel and the nominal end of the walk, on the main A170 (SE515829). There are, however, a number of possible diversions for those who have arrived here with time to spare. A few hundred yards to the right is the top of Sutton Bank, right on the edge of the escarpment and with a magnificent panorama including Great Whernside, 32 miles away in the Pennines, Ripon and Knaresborough. Closer at hand are Gormire Lake, supposed to be bottomless and cradled at the foot of Whitestone Cliff, and, to the south, Roulston Scar and the detached cone of Hood Hill.

The drove road can be traced for some distance to the south, past Scotch Corner to Oldstead, where the drovers chose between routes leading to the markets at York and Malton. And a final diversion could take in the village of Kilburn, notable for John ('Mousy') Thompson's furniture workshops, and the Kilburn White Horse on the slopes above the village. First cut in 1857, it forms a conspicuous landmark from the surrounding lowlands. The Cleveland Way can then be followed round Roulston Scar and back to the top of Sutton Bank.

Notes

Maps   OS 1:25,000 Outdoor Leisure sheet 26 (North York Moors – West) or 1:50,000 sheet 100.

Further reading   Malcolm Boyes, *A Guide to the Cleveland Way* (Constable, 1977); Harry Mead, *Inside the North York Moors* (David & Charles, 1978).

Public transport   Osmotherley has a two-hourly service from North-allerton, the Hambleton Hotel a much less frequent service on Friday, Saturday, Sunday and Monday to Thirsk (two or three buses on each of these days). Thirsk and Northallerton are connected by reasonably frequent trains.

The course of High Street in the Trout Beck valley, with the Ill Bell range to the right

29

THE OLD CRAVEN WAY

Dent to Ingleton 11 miles/18km

A walk of contrasts traversing the slopes of one of the 'Three Peaks' of North Yorkshire. Dent, prettified for tourism, is soon left behind and the Old Craven Way is followed as it contours around the eastern slopes of Whernside. The long southern ridge passes limestone pavements and swallow holes to reach its climax at Twistleton Scar End, a white cliff perched above Ingleton.

Historical Background

At first sight the Old Craven Way appears to be a road of supremely little consequence. It runs between Dent, a tiny village remotely situated to the east of Sedbergh, and Ingleton, almost equally small and off the beaten track. Yet both places were once much more important and were thriving industrial centres, Dent as the centre of the stocking-knitting trade and the place where 'Dent marble' was quarried, and Ingleton as the site of cotton mills, a tannery, limestone quarries and even a short-lived coal mine.

Inevitably a track was beaten out between the two towns, and instead of using Kingsdale it kept to the higher ground to the east of Whernside. Its origin appears to be early medieval – the road from Dent to Ingleton, then called Craven's Wath or Little Craven's Wald, is cited in a dispute over the boundary between Newby and Dent – and its first users were trains of packhorses.

The two alternative names quoted above for the road by no means exhaust the possibilities. It has also been called Craven's Old Way, Cravens Way and, more recently, the Old Craven Way. In contouring around Whernside it provided ready access at a later date to the coal seams which were worked by means of primitive bell-shaped pits until well into the nineteenth century, and for the transport of the coal (and quicklime produced at nearby limekilns) to Dent and Ingleton.

After passing along the eastern flanks of Whernside the Old Craven Way

The drove road on the northern slopes of Kailzie Hill

The cobbled main street of Dent

descended from Ellerbeck into Chapel le Dale and then followed the minor road past Beezleys to Ingleton. This section almost certainly re-uses the Roman road between Brough, in Wensleydale, and Ingleton, although there is no evidence at all that the Romans used the route north of Chapel le Dale. Equally there is little proof that the direct way south from Ellerbeck, now known as Kirby Gate, was used by the packhorses, though it seems highly probable. Kirby Gate (and its western twin, the Turbary Road on the eastern slopes of Gragareth) is best known as a peat-cutters' road, of purely local significance, but it continues the line of the Old Craven Way much more directly to Ingleton and must surely have seen considerable traffic in medieval times.

Description of the Route

Dent is either a marvellous place to begin the walk or a nightmare from which it is marvellous to escape, according to one's taste. In his *Portrait of the Pennines*, Redfern describes it as 'a village almost out of this world in unspoilt charm'; Harry Rée suggests that it 'has become a show village . . . of course, if you like your villages to look like the opening scene of a pantomime, then Dent on a fine day is for you'.

Naturally a great deal depends upon the time of year – and even the time of day – at which Dent is visited. At the height of summer it appears self-

186

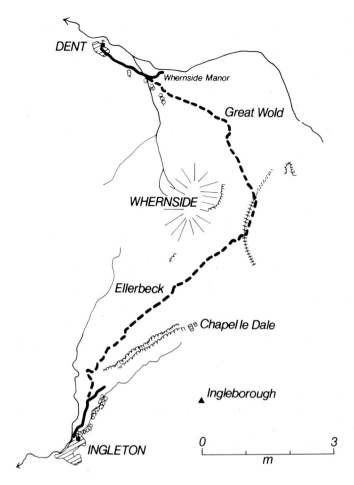

consciously pretty, its cobbled streets an artificially preserved tourist attraction; at quieter times the place can be savoured at leisure. The memorial to the geologist Adam Sedgwick, who was born here, and the church attract most visitors, but in a way the greater attraction of the place is its record of continuous settlement from its origins as a Norse hamlet through its busiest times as a centre of the knitting industry in the eighteenth and nineteenth centuries (in 1800 packhorse trains from Kendal collected 800 pairs of stockings a week) to the discovery and working of 'Dent marble', actually a limestone, from 1810 onwards, and finally to its present status as a tourist honeypot.

To escape from Dent (SD705871) along the Old Craven Way take the lane heading south-east past Howgill House to the great, square Georgian edifice of Whernside Manor. Just before the house, which is now an outdoor centre, take the 'no through road' on the right and then go left on to a bridleway after 200 yards. Bear right after a field gate and begin the only real climb on the Craven Way, along a fine green lane sandwiched between limestone walls.

Pause on the struggle up to Whernside's Great Wold to survey the scene. There is a superb view of Dentdale, backed by the blue-green Howgill Fells, and to their left is Deepdale and the curious hollow known as Combe Bottom. A little more climbing brings the Settle to Carlisle railway line into view to the east. The site of Dent's former station, 4 miles from the village, can be picked out, and unless the determined rearguard action against the line's intended closure (announced in 1983 but withdrawn in 1984, at least for five years) is finally successful the line as a whole will become no more than a silent monument to former times.

At a boggy section near the Horse Well the right-hand wall reappears and the Old Craven Way resumes the character of a green field lane. The enclosures on the right look oddly out of place on this windswept hillside, but the map indicates 'old pits' and there was some sporadic coal-working here. The lane continues along the spring line, passing Old Wife's Well, Thorough Men Springs and several others. A derelict limekiln and long-abandoned little limestone quarry over on the left explain the need for coal as a fuel – for the long, slow burn which produced quicklime.

Opposite the kiln a faint track leads past Whernside Tarns, a pleasant group of little pools with a fine outlook, to the summit of Whernside, at 2,415ft (736m) the highest of the Three Peaks (the others are Penyghent and Ingleborough) though to most people by far the least imposing. But the ascent is a long, uninteresting grind and the old road to Ingleton is much to be preferred.

Keep on, then, along the Old Craven Way as it curves round the north-east flank of Whernside, contouring at around 1,600ft, as far as Duncan Sike Foot, then climbing along the little gill of that name and swinging right alongside peat banks to reach the road's highest point of 1,770ft (540m) on Craven Wold. The descent is dead straight, down Grain Ings and past Force Gill with its memorable cascading waterfalls to pass under the railway. The lane sticks close to the railway, then dives underneath it again to reach Winterscales.

Winterscales is the first of a string of farms perched on a wide grassy shelf above the Winterscales Beck but well below the brooding, inhospitable summit plateau of Whernside. The farms date from the Norse invasions, as the names themselves – Ellerbeck, Bruntscar, Ivescar, Winterscales and so on – make clear. Later several of them became grange farms belonging to the great monasteries. Notable features on this part of the journey are the fine bridge at Winterscales Farm, the caves at Ivescar and Bruntscar, and Hodge Hole, an old barn at Two Gills Foot.

At Ellerbeck the main route of the Old Craven Way swings left past Gillhead to the tiny chapel of St Leonard at Chapel le Dale, then follows the minor road on the west side of the River Doe all the way to Ingleton. This is a

Whernside from the limestone pavement above Twistleton Scar. The Craven Way, here also known as Kirby Gate, carves a curving course through the exposed limestone

fine walk, not too heavily trafficked, and it follows the course not just of a packhorse route but also of the former Roman road from Ingleton to the Roman fort at Brough, near Hawes. But my preference is to keep to the hills and trace the course of Kirby Gate – itself probably a summer version of the packhorse track – to Twistleton Scar End and Ingleton.

Southwards from Ellerbeck the track across the moor is none too clear as it climbs obliquely below West Fell. Slowly it becomes more obvious as it passes between swallow holes, some with beautiful fluted rock formations; on the ridge above a continuous wall should be visible, and if all else fails this can be followed all the way down.

A glance back reveals the surprisingly shapely southern aspect of Whernside. To the left is Ingleborough, its summit cone rising dramatically above the surrounding moorland, and beyond Kingsdale on the right the peat-cutters' Turbary Road can be picked out on the slopes of Gragareth. Ahead the walk becomes steadily more interesting as it passes and eventually carves its way through limestone pavements on Ewes Top. The 'pavements' were originally huge flat sheets of limestone, but rain has eroded them along lines of weakness which have become deep, intersecting fissures separating the remaining blocks of limestone.

Disused railway viaduct, Ingleton

Kirby Gate, now marked by occasional cairns, descends to the edge of Twistleton Scar, then uses an excellent green ledge as it zigzags down the limestone cliff. The green path leads down to a gated minor road, Twistleton Lane, where – improbably enough – an ice-cream van may be parked in summer. Follow Twistleton Lane past the crumbling remains of the old inn at Scar End to the 'Roman' road less than a mile north of Ingleton.

Having lost its railways, its cotton mill and its coal mine, Ingleton (SD695732) now relies on quarrying (one massive example, across the River Doe, intrudes into the scene during the descent of Kirby Gate) and tourism. It is a likeable if unremarkable place, with a fine pub, the Craven Heifer, a cluster of grey stone cottages and a much restored church whose nave has had to be rebuilt twice because of subsidence. And, if the time is available, the second of the Three Peaks, Ingleborough, is within easy reach . . .

Notes

Maps OS 1:25,000 Outdoor Leisure sheet 2 (The Three Peaks) or 1:50,000 sheet 98.

Further reading Arthur Raistrick, *Green Roads in the Mid Pennines* (Moorland, 1978); Harry Rée and Caroline Forbes, *The Three Peaks of Yorkshire* (Wildwood House, 1983).

Public transport Dent has an almost non-existent public transport service – one bus on Wednesday mornings from Kendal. Conversely, Ingleton is well served by buses along the A65 from Skipton and it is also fairly close to Bentham rail station on the Leeds to Lancaster line.

30

HIGH STREET

Tirril to Troutbeck 16 miles/26km

A magnificent but demanding high-level ridge walk along the High Street range, the easternmost ridge in the Lake District and one which derives its name from the Roman road which follows the entire length of the ridge.

Historical Background

The Lake District lay on the extreme edge of the Roman Empire. There is no evidence that the Romans exploited the mineral wealth of the area, considerable though this was, and they certainly had little interest in settling or developing it. Nevertheless, when they first reached the area at the end of the first century AD, the Romans built a chain of forts and a series of connecting roads in order to ensure their continued control of the district.

The most impressive of the Roman forts in the Lake District is Hardknott Castle, perched on a spur overlooking the valley of Eskdale, but the most awe-inspiring of the roads is undoubtedly High Street. Connecting the forts of Brocavum, near Penrith, and Galava, on the shores of Lake Windermere near Ambleside, this celebrated road traverses one of the major ridges of the Lake District, rising to over 2,700ft. Despite its lack of strategic importance, this is an outstanding example of Roman audacity.

Yet the ridge route is older still: the road was described as the *Brethestrete* (Briton's street) in the thirteenth century, a clear indication that the Romans had merely adapted an existing trackway – one which neolithic man may have used to distribute the stone axes from the 'factory' in Langdale. Much later, in medieval times, Scots border raiders found the road invaluable for their cattle rustling, and part of it came to be known as the Scot Rake.

Description of the Route

The exact course of the Roman road is uncertain at first, but the route has been traced south–west from Tirril (across fields, so a detour along the B5320 is necessary) to Celleron Farm (NY496252). Keep straight ahead at Celleron, then bear right to pass Winder Hall and skirt the limestone summit of Heughscar Hill, with wide views of the Scottish hills and the Pennines. The

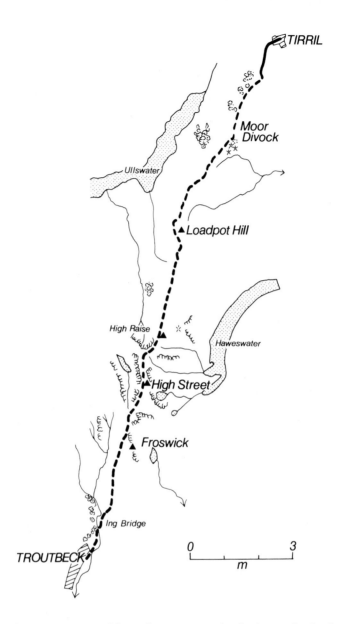

Roman road is represented here by a green track through the bracken as far as the junction with a wide track from Pooley Bridge to Heltonhead.

Now the Roman road, of which there are few traces underfoot, crosses Moor Divock, an area littered with prehistoric remains and clearly highly important in the Bronze Age. A wet and deeply rutted path leads to the Cockpit, with some sixty-five stones – only one of them upright – demarcating the site of a stone circle. To the east of the Cockpit is an unusual and impressive cairn circle, and further towards Heltonhead is the Cop Stone, a broad and isolated 5ft monolith. The whole area is pockmarked with tumuli and other unexplained mounds and hollows.

At the Cockpit the Roman road alters course to the south-west; the exact line of the path is sometimes obscure in places as it slowly rises away from Moor Divock. However, the same general direction is maintained across the bare slopes of Barton Fell, with Arthur's Pike and Bonscale Pike well to the right. Very gradually the path, which is now much clearer on the ground, gains height past a series of boundary stones.

The Roman road continues towards Loadpot Hill, passing the Standing Stone, now isolated but once part of a stone circle, and the gloomy hollow of Loadpot Hole. On these northern slopes of Loadpot Hill a section of the road was excavated, revealing a complex method of construction: 8in layers of peat and gravel resting on a 2ft thick bed of quarried boulders. Nowadays the antiquity of the route is not at all obvious, although it is still used as a quick way south to High Street.

The summit of Loadpot Hill is a dull grassy expanse, and unfortunately the one special feature of the hill now lies in ruins. This is Lowther House, a shooting lodge belonging to the Lowther estate, dramatically placed in an exposed location north of the col between Loadpot Hill and its similarly rounded and grassy neighbour, Wether Hill. After its original use had ceased, the majority of the lodge was pulled down, but the stone fireplace and tall chimney stack remained as an unmistakable landmark. Exposure to Lakeland wind, snow and frost exacted a severe toll, however, and most of the structure collapsed in 1973: the rubble decorates the surrounding fellside.

The col south of the Lowther House chimney separates the Fusedale Beck on the right from the little-known valley of Cawdale Beck on the left. A series of deep peat groughs, somewhat similar in character to those near the packhorse route across the Dark Peak, now has to be negotiated, before the ground rises slowly to the summit of Wether Hill. A small cairn and a wooden stake mark the summit.

The road is now absolutely obvious along the narrowing ridge to the summit plateau of High Raise, the second highest mountain in the High Street range. Possibly out of respect for this superior altitude there is a rash of boulders around the summit cairn, which is itself much larger than those encountered so far along the course of the Roman road. The road itself passes slightly west of the summit and continues around the rim of the crags above the valley of Rampsgill Beck. The line of crags enclosing the valley head is particularly impressive.

Keep close to the edge of the plateau and climb gently up to the summit of Rampsgill Head, marked by a somewhat ruinous cairn. To the north of the summit is a fine view along the Rampsgill valley, with Ullswater beyond and the Helvellyn and Fairfield ridges on the western horizon. The route now

The course of the Roman road on the summit plateau of High Street

drops slightly to the Straits of Riggindale, where the ridge is at its narrowest. The Roman road now inclines towards the western edge of the ridge, though without the daring indicated on OS maps, which over-dramatise the rather minor crags nearby.

The rutted track following the Roman route is all too visible as it rises gradually across the grassy plateau, although it is hardly recognisable as an ancient trackway. Nevertheless it offers silent testimony to the achievement of the Romans in forcing the road through the sodden peat at this remarkable altitude. The triangulation column marking the top of High Street itself (2,718ft/828m) lies away to the left of the path, and the sight of it is a timely reminder of the difficulties which must have accompanied the construction of the road across this boggy waste.

South of the summit pillar a wall marks the crest of the ridge, and the Roman road gradually approaches and then joins the wall, and finally parts company when the wall abruptly turns to descend the fellside. Past Thornthwaite Crag, with its 14ft beacon tower, the road keeps to the ridge, but instead of climbing towards the next peak, Froswick, it bears right to descend into the Troutbeck valley. The route down into the valley is quite steep – the average gradient is about 1 in 5 – and Margary has suggested that this would have ruled out the use of the route by vehicular traffic.

This slanting descent is known as Scot Rake because border cattle raiders used the Roman route for their incursions during the medieval period. The rake, a green track standing out prominently in the bracken, slopes down quickly to a gate leading towards the rough track down the valley. This track follows Hagg Gill downstream, past a pair of overgrown tumuli and then, across the stream, a huge quarry which has given the fellside here the name of Quarry Brow.

The Roman road leads down Hagg Gill towards Troutbeck Park, a medieval deer park which became a statesman farm, and which was once owned by Beatrix Potter. The route turns away from it, however, by taking the signposted footpath to the left, crossing a field, and rejoining the track along the flat valley floor of the Trout Beck past Ing Bridge. Shortly beyond the

The Trout Beck valley and the Ill Bell range from the path following the course of the Roman road

The statesman farmhouse of Town End, Troutbeck

bridge the road curves right, but a footpath continues straight ahead through the trees to the main road (A592). The lane opposite heads for the centre of the straggling collection of statesman farms which make up the village of Troutbeck (NY413028). The National Trust's showpiece farmhouse of Town End, the attractive clusters of farms around a series of wells, and the Queen's Head, with its historic Mayor's Parlour and its real ale, make this an especially welcoming village after the rigours of the High Street range.

> **Notes**
>
> **Maps**   OS 1;25,000 Outdoor Leisure sheets 5 and 7 (The Lake District – North-East and South-East) or 1in Tourist Map (The Lake District).
> **Further reading**   Michael Dunn, *Walking through the Lake District* (David & Charles, 1984); Geoffrey Berry, *Across Northern Hills* (Westmorland Gazette, 1975); Ivan Margary, *Roman Roads in Britain* (John Baker, 3rd edn. 1973).
> **Public transport**   Tirril is served by the Penrith to Patterdale bus service, with six buses a day in each direction on weekdays, but Troutbeck has a bus service in high summer only, and then only on Tuesdays and Thursdays, to Ambleside (but both Ambleside and Windermere can quickly be reached on foot).

31

CLENNELL STREET

Circular walk from Alwinton 18 miles/29km

This is one of the best walks in the book – 18 miles of exhilarating walking on excellent paths and tracks in the Cheviot Hills, following ancient border routes which have been used through the centuries by raiding parties, cattle rustlers, drovers, whisky smugglers and others. Mainly because of public transport limitations it has been devised as a circular walk based on Alwinton in upper Coquetdale; the route ascends Clennell Street to the Border fence, turns west along the border for a mile, and then follows The Street (or Clattering Path) back down to the Coquet valley.

Historical Background

The border tracks leading across the Cheviots from the Tweed valley to Redesdale and Coquetdale date from prehistoric times and have played a crucial part in the turbulent history of the region. The Romans converted one such route into part of Dere Street, which ran between Corbridge and Jedburgh, and the Roman road later became an important medieval route (Gamel's Path) and then a major drove route. Further east, ancient tracks connected the headwaters of the Coquet with the valleys of the Kale and Bowmont Waters: The Street led from Slyme Foot to Hownam, Clennell Street from Alwinton to Yetholm, and the Salter's Road (also known from the thirteenth century as the Thieves Road) from Alnham to its junction with Clennell Street on the border ridge.

There is clear evidence for the antiquity of these routes, from the hill-forts at Clennell near Alwinton and the Roman camp at Chew Green, where Dere Street meets the Border, to early-medieval documentary references – Clennell Street, for example, is described as 'the great road of Yarnspath' in a charter dated 1181.

Clennell Street itself – the best 'street' for walking, since Dere Street passes through army ranges – was never Romanised but may have retained its prehistoric function as a trade route linking Scotland with the south, and connecting the Northumbrian outposts of the Votadini with their tribal heartland further north. In medieval times it was used by the monks of Newminster to reach their sheep pastures in Kidland, and less honestly by

Alwinton and upper Coquetdale

cattle reivers raiding the Coquet valley during the Border wars.

Later, the route was shared between drovers – travelling south from Falkirk Tryst, and perhaps resting overnight at the stance at Wholehope – and whisky smugglers, who distributed the illicit produce of Rory's Still on the Usway Burn and other clandestine stills hidden in the Cheviot valleys. The droving trade was at its height in the later eighteenth century, when as many as 100,000 cattle a year crossed the border, but the coming of the railways and the improvement of major roads conspired to render the drovers redundant. Whisky smuggling peaked later, in the early nineteenth century, when differential taxes made the risks worth while.

Description of the Route

Alwinton is now the highest village in upper Coquetdale, and still acts as a centre for the social life of the upper valley. The original settlement was at Low Alwinton, now deserted except for St Michael's church, imposingly sited on steep ground above the river, and famous for the ten steps which separate nave and chancel. Now the village lies further north, with a cluster of low cottages, a shop and a pub, the Rose and Thistle, close to an open green by the Hosedon Burn. The Alwinton Show, a traditional shepherds' meet held in October, is the highlight of the year and the best-known such show in Northumberland, with sheepdog trials, hound-trailing and wrestling included in the programme.

Cross the Hosedon Burn on a footbridge east of the village green (NT921063) and turn north (signposted Clennell Street) on a track which rises between two farms to the open fell. The track skirts a rounded hill which has obvious traces of the ditches of an Iron Age hill-fort amongst its rock outcrops, and on a hill across the deep Alwin valley is the site of another settlement. Here is a first indication of the antiquity of Clennell Street, which was important enough to be protected by two hill-forts in prehistoric times.

To the right, in the wooded valley of the River Alwin, is Clennell Hall, much altered but incorporating a fourteenth-century pele-tower. The hall is the only survivor of a deserted medieval village, which was destroyed and converted to a sheep run in the sixteenth century, and this, together with traces of medieval cultivation terraces above the former village and on Lord's Seat, to the left of Clennell Street, is evidence of the intensive medieval settlement of the area, which now consists only of a high sheepwalk.

Clennell Street climbs slowly on to the ridge between the Alwin and the Alwinton Burn, passing yet another settlement and an inconspicuous cross-

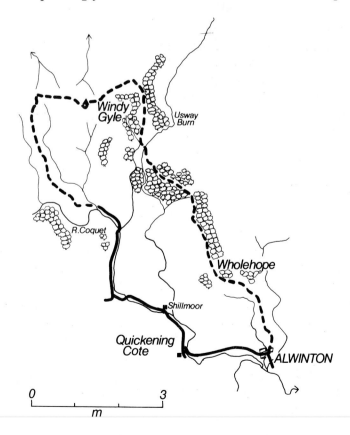

dyke, probably constructed in the sixteenth century to block the return of Scots raiders along the ancient road. There is an excellent prospect southwards over Coquetdale to the Simonside Hills, and now the view ahead and to the right also begins to open out, embracing Kidland Forest, now almost entirely the conifer-ridden preserve of the Forestry Commission, which owns more than 6,000 acres, but once a monastic sheep pasture. Newminster Abbey, founded near Morpeth in 1157, held the grazing rights of Kidland Manor by 1181 and within a century had 18,000 sheep grazing the north side of upper Coquetdale. One of the medieval boundary walls of this Cistercian estate can be seen ascending the hillside near Windyhaugh.

Clennell Street continues northwards as an obvious track which descends to a gate in a slightly boggy hollow (the first of many stells – circular sheepfolds characteristic of the Cheviots – is down in the valley on the left) then climbs steadily, skirting a young plantation, to the forlorn ruins of Wholehope, once a shepherds' cottage and later a youth hostel. Now it is virtually demolished, and the remains of the cattle park used by the drovers on their way south are more interesting.

Beyond a gate the track enters the forest, and since the conifers hide the view the next mile offers a stretch of relatively dull but fast high-level walking. The track becomes a forestry road and, during a brief respite from the trees, a stony track over open moorland. Clennell Street bears right, contours round a minor hill, descends into an infant valley and is then enveloped by the trees again. At least the trees are younger, the track is wide and green, and the bird song and pine fragrance compensate for the loss of open views.

In another ½ mile the forest track swings sharp left, and it is vital to keep straight on (a signpost would not come amiss here) along an intermittent path on peat. Leave the forest by crossing a dilapidated stile, then press on (the path is not immediately obvious) to cross a small stream and descend by means of an excellent green rake to the valley of the Usway Burn.

The stream is much larger than expected, with deep pools and a miniature waterfall below a sturdy footbridge. Another stell is located immediately upstream, but the route climbs diagonally up the river cliff, then makes for a track coming up Middle Hill towards the farm at Uswayford. This area of 'the Middle' was the site of an important medieval junction of tracks, and there was a drovers' inn and a cockpit in this remote spot. Higher up the Usway Burn, beyond the waterfall of Davidson's Linn, was Rory's Still, where whisky was illegally distilled for the benefit of drovers, shepherds and smugglers using Clennell Street and the Salter's Road.

The former course of Clennell Street is marked by a particularly fine holloway which descends by means of a pronounced zigzag to cross the

Clennell Hall (far left) and Clennell Street

Barrow Burn near another stell; but it is easier to make for the main track to Uswayford, and then to turn left to climb Hazely Law on a fair track threatened by the encroaching plantations.

The track climbing Hazely Law was known in medieval times as Hexpethgate. Just south of the Border it is joined by the Salter's Road and the two climb across peat hags and heather to the border fence at Cocklawgate. To the east the Cheviot itself is prominent; Clennell Street goes straight on into Scotland, descending Outer Cock Law to the valley of the Bowmont Water; but this walk heads left, following the Pennine Way – described as 'undefined' on the map, but beaten out into a wide damp path across the peat.

The path ascends to the summit of Windy Gyle (2,032ft/619m), with its enormous summit cairn and fine views east to the Cheviot and north into Scotland. Here the Wardens of the Marches came on medieval days of truce, and here is Russell's Cairn, commemorating Lord Francis Russell, killed by Sir John Forster at one of the most turbulent of these Border trysts, in 1585.

Keep to the border fence south, then west, from Windy Gyle (though a short-cut omits the southerly diversion) and after a mile or so turn left, on to the ridge of Black Braes. This is the narrow ridge dividing the Carlcroft and Rowhope Burns which carries the ancient track of The Street (the eighteenth-century Clattering Path) on its journey south from Hownam. The Street is especially well marked on the slow descent of Black Braes, and close to the border it negotiates two cross-dykes, possibly sixteenth century in origin and clearly designed to check travellers along the old highway.

The way down The Street is exhilaratingly fast, on close-cropped turf across Hindside Knowe to the Coquet at Slyme Foot, where the track from Rowhope comes in from the left. Here there was an inn in the eighteenth century, and Dippie Dixon reported in *Upper Coquetdale*, published in 1904, that it was 'the resort of all the neighbouring sheep farmers, who used to spend their time drinking and gambling'.

Sadly the rest of the walk has to use the valley road, although the scenery of upper Coquetdale is excellent and there is little traffic (a good deal of what there is tends to be military, since all the southern slopes are part of the Redesdale artillery range). The road leads past Barrowburn, where the Newminster monks had a fulling mill, and Windyhaugh, where – astonishingly – there is a primary school catering for the children of the sheep farms in the upper valley.

For the next mile or so the valley is empty, with just a few MOD warning notices and the Coquet in its rocky trench. Beyond Bygate Hall lies Shillmoor, an attractive Georgian farmhouse serving as a reminder of the resettlement of the valley after the end of the Border raids. Less than a mile down the valley is Quickening Cote, now taken over by the military but once the site of the hamlet of Aldenscheles. The site of the little settlement and its thirteenth-century chapel is marked by low mounds near the confluence of the Coquet and Ridlees Burn at Linshiels.

The road now leads directly to Alwinton and the end of an outstanding walk in the relatively unfrequented Northumberland National Park. And as a final bonus, the Rose and Thistle, a superb traditional pub with no frills but bursting with character, now sells real ale straight from the barrel; a marvellous end to a classic walk.

Notes

Map   OS 1:50,000 sheet 80.
Further reading   F. R. Banks, *The Borders* (Batsford, 1977); Countryside Commission, *Northumberland National Park Guide* (HMSO, 1969); Robert Newton, *The Northumberland Landscape* (Hodder & Stoughton, 1972).
Public transport   None.
Accommodation   Very scarce, although some of the farms in upper Coquetdale, such as Uswayford and Rowhope, offer bed and breakfast. More varied accommodation is available in Rothbury.

32

DROVE ROADS
IN SOUTHERN SCOTLAND

Peebles to Tibbie Shiels Inn 14 miles/22km

From the middle of the eighteenth century, when Falkirk supplanted Crieff as the main 'tryst' or collecting centre for Scottish cattle, drove roads threaded their way through the southern uplands towards the Pennines and the Tyne valley in Northumberland. This exhilaratingly open walk starts at the King's Muir in Peebles, a notable cattle stance, and follows one of the most important routes south past Dryhope Tower to the Tibbie Shiels Inn at the head of St Mary's Loch, with an optional extension to Teviothead, south of Hawick.

Historical Background

For centuries the economy of the Highlands was centred upon the rearing of cattle and sheep and their sale at the major markets or trysts. There is evidence that Scots cattle were being driven south to England by the fifteenth century, but it was not until around 1770, by which time Falkirk had supplanted Crieff as the most important tryst in Scotland, that English cattle-buyers became predominant.

The gentle, rounded hills of the Southern Uplands held no terrors for drovers who had in many cases negotiated long, exposed routes through the Highland glens, and hence there is no great concentration of drove roads into the easiest territory. The drovers had widely varying destinations, so that an intricate network of routes was quickly established, generally heading south towards the Cheviots and then the Pennines or the Tyne valley in Northumberland.

Probably the most important through route was the drove road from Falkirk to Peebles, Teviothead and the Cheviots. Once sold at the tryst at Falkirk, the cattle would be driven to Bathgate and Mid Calder, then over the Pentland Hills by way of the pass known as the Cauldstane Slap, down to West Linton and Romannobridge – where a toll had to be paid at the Romanno tollbar – and across the Cloich Hills to Peebles. Rights of common grazing have existed on the King's Muir, beside the River Tweed at Peebles, since 1506.

A number of alternatives existed south of Peebles: across Birkscairn Hill to Dryhope, Buccleuch and Teviothead; to Traquair and up the valley of the Quair Water to join the first route at Dryhope; or across the famous Minchmoor Road to Selkirk, thence to Hawick or Buccleuch. The road over the Minch Muir, past the Cheese Well and Brown Knowe to Philiphaugh and Selkirk, was used in the thirteenth century by the monks of Kelso Abbey, in 1296 by Edward I, and in 1645 by Montrose after his defeat at the Battle of Philiphaugh. From both Hawick and Teviothead routes existed to Newcastleton and then to the Tyne valley.

Description of the Route

The starting point of the walk is the Royal Burgh of Peebles, granted its royal charter in 1367 by David II but with a much longer history. St Mungo is supposed to have visited Peebles in the sixth century, and David I had a royal castle here in the twelfth century. Now it is a typically bustling Borders town with a wide main street spreading eastwards from the kirk, itself built over the site of David's castle. Spaced along High Street are Bank House, formerly the home of John Buchan, Parliament Square (where an emergency session of the Scots parliament was held in 1346), the excellent early-nineteenth-century Tontine Hotel and the Chambers Institution, the nineteenth-century home of the Edinburgh publishing family best known for their dictionaries.

For the most scenic introduction to the drove road seek out the alley leading down from the High Street just to the west of the Chambers Institution (NT253404), follow this down to Tweed Green – the fine Tweed Bridge is away to the right – and cross the river on a pedestrian footbridge. Keep straight on across Victoria Park to join Springhill Road and turn left, climbing gently away from the town. The park was once part of the King's Muir, where the rights of common grazing date back to a charter confirmed by James IV in 1506; so too, for that matter, was the land now occupied by the undistinguished housing estate a little further south.

Springhill Road becomes Glen Road, at first still an access road for housing estates, but later a narrow drive between avenues of trees with the large Haystoun estate to the right. The way ahead abruptly becomes a stony track enclosed between young trees, then after a green farm lane goes off left down to Whitehaugh a signpost indicates a 'public footpath by Gypsy Glen to Yarrow'. Slither down the often muddy slope ahead into Gypsy Glen, cross the Haystoun Burn on a modern footbridge, and climb the opposite slope to emerge from the trees into open countryside, with wide views.

The drove road quickly assumes its characteristic form as a wide green lane between low drystone walls, although at first there are wire fences in

Tweed Bridge, Peebles

PEEBLES

R.Tweed

Cardrona
Forest

▲ Birkscairn
Hill

Stake ▲
Law

Twr

Dryhope
Tower

St Mary's
Loch

TIBBIE SHIELS INN

0   3
                m

The drove road on the northern slopes of Kailzie Hill

places and a good deal of its width is obscured by bushes and assorted encroaching undergrowth. The total width is impressive, however, not least as a reminder of the sheer volume of four-footed traffic which came this way at the height of the droving trade. Now comes the first serious ascent, as the drove road passes through a little wood and climbs to a gate. There are fine views from here back along the line of the drove to the Tweed valley and the wooded grounds of the Peebles Hydro, the largest hotel in the Borders.

A second but less exacting climb ensues, on a track which, though it is sometimes deeply rutted, generally picks the best ground between the widely separated containing walls. The way lies through a field populated, on all my visits, with excessively nervous cattle, and past the sad remains of fallen trees, to a second gate where a halt to survey the magnificent scenery is essential.

To the north lies the town of Peebles in its hollow at the confluence of the Tweed and a number of its tributaries. West, across the valley of the Glensax Burn (better seen a little later on in the walk) are the thickly wooded hills beyond the upper Tweed, and to the east – where the lower course of the Tweed is again a significant feature – the old ruined tower near Glentress stands in front of the little-known hills around Windlestraw Law and Deaf Heights.

The drove road, now contained between a solid wall to the left and its dilapidated twin on the right, contours round a minor hill at the end of the ridge, negotiates a sharp dip beyond a third gate, then adopts a classic ridgeway form, now with the Glensax valley stretching away into the distance on the right and the jagged edge of Juniper Crags prominent beyond the Glensax trench.

No sooner has the pattern of a walled ridgeway been established, however, than the walls disappear and the drove road is left to make its way across a heather moor towards Kailzie Hill. At times the heather has recolonised part of the track, and the drove, once so wide, has been reduced to a single-width path. The Sitka spruce of Cardrona Forest begins to intrude to the left, reaching almost up to the ridge line, but Kailzie Hill itself is largely unaffected and there is an excellent prospect northwards along the Glensax valley from a prominent cairn.

At first the route ahead is obvious, between the conifers to the left and steeply sloping ground to the right, to the cairn on Kirkhope Law; and navigation thereafter is aided by the arrival of a wire fence, though on the way to Birkscairn Hill the ground near to the fence is boggy in places. The drovers by-passed the summit of Birkscairn Hill and continued roughly south (take care to leave the ridge instead of ploughing on south-west alongside the fence to Stake Law and Dun Rig), contouring around the head of the Quair Water valley at about 1,600ft. Down to the right is the often wild water of Loch Eddy.

The drove road can now readily be followed past Whiteknowe Head down to the cleft of the Douglas Burn and then to Blackhouse Tower, now a remote and forlorn ruin but boasting an extraordinary history. Its remoteness is deceptive, for this area was once the most heavily populated part of Ettrick Forest, and Blackhouse was the seat of the Douglas barony. By 1057 Sir John Douglas was baron here; much later the 'Douglas tragedy' saw the elder daughter of the house, who had eloped with a neighbouring laird, pursued by her father and his seven sons, all of whom were slain by the laird.

The Glensax drove road is joined at Blackhouse by one of the drovers' routes from Traquair, and the two go forward across the green and gentle flanks of South Hawkshaw Rig as the Southern Upland Way, the newest of Scotland's small and by no means universally welcomed band of long-distance footpaths. Undoubtedly it would be regrettable if the Southern Upland Way suffered from footpath erosion to the same extent as parts of the West Highland Way, though in any case the Blackhouse drove road, after all the traffic it has seen, would probably survive unscathed.

The drove road converges with the Dryhope Burn, with the first glimpses of St Mary's Loch in its hollow between rounded hills. At a gate the route lies to the left, following the Southern Upland Way along a new path to the A708 instead of tramping through the hamlet of Dryhope. Half a field away are the substantial remains of Dryhope Tower, an excellent example of a fortified Border house. Mary Scott, known as the 'flower of Yarrow' and an ancestor of Sir Walter Scott, was born here.

Cross the A708 and keep to the path leading around the south-eastern shores of St Mary's Loch, well away from the main road. No path is shown on the map further south than Bowerhope, but in fact the lake shore can be followed below Bowerhope Law all the way to the Tibbie Shiels Inn (NT241206). The Loch of the Lowes, separated from St Mary's Loch by a flat area created from the alluvial deposits of the Oxcleuch and Crosscleuch Burns, was once part of the larger lake; now the connecting stream is crossed by a fine narrow road bridge, leading back to the main road and the bus to Selkirk.

The Continuation to Teviothead

The section south of St Mary's Loch is equally full of interest, but only the strongest of walkers will be able to complete the whole route in a day. Follow the eastern shore of the Loch of the Lowes to the end of a wood, then strike up over Pikestone Rig and take the left-hand track, the Kirk Road, to Ettrick church. Keep travelling east to Deephope and Buccleuch, then walk past Kingside Loch (where a wide culvert transports the drove road over a stream) and Muselee, and take the wide track south to Dryden Fell and Teviothead.

Notes

Maps   OS 1:50,000 sheets 73 and 79.
Further reading   K. M. Andrew and A. A. Thrippleton, *The Southern Uplands* (Scottish Mountaineering Club, 1976); A. R. B. Haldane, *The Drove Roads of Scotland* (repub. David & Charles, 1973); D. G. Moir, *Scottish Hill Tracks: 1. Southern Scotland* (Bartholomew, 1975).
Accommodation   There is plenty of choice in Peebles, but further south few possibilities exist. For those contemplating the longer walk described there are inns at St Mary's Loch and also the excellent Gordon Arms Hotel, 2 miles east of Dryhope. At Teviothead accommodation is very scarce, although there is bed and breakfast available at Coltscleuch.
Public transport   Peebles has an hourly service from Edinburgh and connections from the other Borders towns. There is a bus service on Thursdays only from Selkirk to St Mary's Loch. Teviothead is on the Edinburgh to Carlisle bus route, with five buses a day in each direction.

33

THE MOUNTH ROAD

Ballater to Invermark 12 miles/19km

The Braes of Angus, formerly known as the Mounth, form neglected but highly rewarding mountain country, and the ancient hill-tracks which connect Deeside and the Angus glens make exploration especially easy. The selected walk traces the course of the Mounth Road itself, sometimes referred to as the Mount Keen track, from Ballater to Glen Esk at Invermark.

Historical Background

The Central Highlands of Scotland essentially consist of two mountain systems, known in early Celtic times as Drumalban and the Monadh or Mounth. Drumalban, the 'backbone' of Scotland, extends from Ben Lomond to Ben Hope in Sutherland; near the Drumochter Pass it throws off a transverse ridge, the Mounth, which (with its northward extension, the high Cairngorms) declines gradually eastwards to reach the North Sea at Tullos Hill near Aberdeen.

The Mounth – the name means 'heathy hills' – is dissected into a series of ridges and deep glens, and is now generally referred to as the southern Cairngorms or the Braes of Angus. The term 'Mounth' tends to be applied only to the splendid series of ancient hill-paths connecting the Angus glens and Strathmore with Deeside to the north, rising in many cases to well over 2,000ft in their passage across a formidable mountain barrier.

All the Mounth tracks have seen a wide variety of travellers, although the most important historically is the Cairn a' Mounth, now the B974 between Banchory and Fettercairn. Macbeth came this way, retreating northwards, in 1057, and in the thirteenth century Edward I marched over the pass. The Mounth Road itself has accommodated cattle and their drovers since at least the sixteenth century, together with monks, pedlars, whisky-smugglers, farmworkers, explorers on horseback (including Queen Victoria) and, most recently, hillwalkers.

Many of the cattle in the early droves had been stolen from Strathmore and were on their way north. Later a more respectable trade grew up, with Black Highland cattle being driven to market in Forfar or Crieff, and in later years Falkirk. The traffic to Falkirk Tryst continued until at least the middle of the nineteenth century, and the southward migration of groups of men and women looking for work during the harvest period persisted later still, almost until 1900.

The southward continuation of the Mounth Road towards Brechin was known in the eighteenth century as the Priest's Road, and even earlier as the Whisky Road. It was used by packhorse trains to convey illicitly distilled whisky from the Highlands to Strathmore, and by the local Episcopalian minister travelling between Invermark and Glen Lethnot. Now it can be followed (though not entirely on the original line) from Invermark through the narrow pass known as the Clash of Wirren to Stonyford, Bridgend and Brechin.

Description of the Route

The Mounth Road departs southwards from Ballater, an attractive Deeside town which was until the 1960s the railhead for Braemar and Balmoral Castle. The original settlement was at Tullich, 2 miles to the east, where the ruined successor to the seventh-century church stands. Ballater itself is an eighteenth-century spa town, developed by Francis Farquharson and his son William in the wake of the 'discovery' in the 1760s that the waters of a spring at Pannaich on the south bank of the River Dee had healing properties. The main north–south shopping street, Bridge Street, is interrupted after a few hundred yards by the Square, an elongated village green on which stands the elegant church of Glenmuick.

Before crossing the Royal Bridge over the Dee it is worth diverting north-east to climb the thickly wooded Craigendarroch ('hill of the oaks'), which not only has magnificent views in both directions along Deeside but also has a splendid southerly prospect towards the north corrie of Lochnagar, the entrance to Glen Muick, and the first stages of the Mounth Road.

Back now to the Royal Bridge (NO372956), opened by Queen Victoria on 6 November 1885 to replace Telford's bridge, swept away in the 'Muckle Spate' of 1829, only twenty years after it had been built. Take the South Deeside Road towards Balmoral (there is a superb view back to Ballater and the Royal Bridge after ¼ mile) as far as the Bridge of Muick. Don't cross the bridge, or even take the minor road leading into Glen Muick; instead follow the track disconcertingly signposted 'Balintober – Private – No Cars'. Despite the absence of any waymarking, this is the beginning of the Mounth Road.

The track is enclosed between hedges and plagued by rabbits for a while, with a glimpse to the right of the ruins of St Nathalan's Chapel, built by the Mackenzies of Glenmuick. On the hill-slopes to the left is the House of Glenmuick, home of the Walker-Okeovers, lairds of Glenmuick, whilst

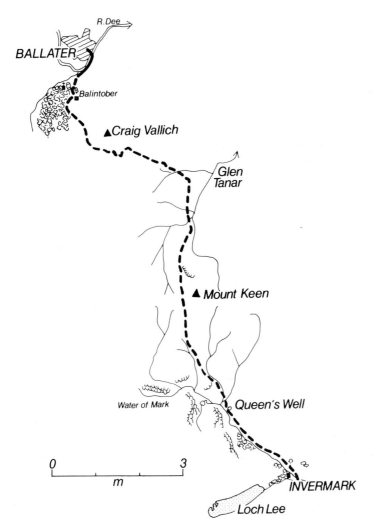

across the River Muick to the right (though not seen until some height has been gained) is the ruined sixteenth-century tower of Knock Castle.

Follow the rough track into a wood and climb past the secluded house of Balintober, then swing left and right to pass through a fragrant pine forest as far as a massive gate which carries a prominent warning: 'This path is dangerous 12 August – 20 October'. Outside the grouse-shooting season the heather moor is likely to be deserted, and the way forward is obvious (indeed, far too obvious) on a deeply scarred Land-Rover track climbing the shoulder of Craig Vallich to the col, marked by small pools, between Craig Vallich and Cairn Leuchan. Across the heavily wooded Glen Muick the summits of the Coyles of Muick, backed by the White Mounth and the forbidding wall of Lochnagar, make an outstanding contribution to the scene.

Keep on roughly eastwards from the col, then swing south to slant down

211

Balintober and the Mounth Road above Bridge of Muick

and cross the Water of Tanar just below the Shiel of Glentanar. Some way downstream is one of the three major surviving remnants of the old Caledonian Forest. The climb out of Glen Tanar is long and quite steep on a spur east of the Black Burn, but after a mile the gradient eases and the Mounth Road passes across the gently sloping western shoulder of Mount Keen at about 2,500ft – though gluttons for punishment can take the left-hand track at the head of the steep slope and continue to the summit (3,077ft/938m).

The two tracks converge south of Mount Keen and make their way, via zigzags and some very steep and quite difficult ground, to the deeply incised valley of the Ladder Burn. Below Glenmark the Water of Mark is reached near the Queen's Well, where a crown-shaped granite monument commemorates the place where Queen Victoria stopped to drink on her ride from Balmoral to Fettercairn in 1861 – only a few weeks before the death of the Prince Consort.

Now the path follows the Water of Mark for 2 miles down to Invermark (a signpost here reassuringly confirms the route to 'Ballater via Mounth' for north-bound walkers). At Invermark (NO443804) are the impressive remains of a four-storied Highland tower, first built in 1526, which acted as an outpost for the Lindsays of Edzell Castle. Here too is a sombre Presbyterian church, dating from 1803, and, after a delightful half-mile stroll beside the River North Esk, Loch Lee in its grimly scenic surroundings.

The Priest's Road: A Continuation to Brechin (16 miles/26km)

Upper Glen Esk, scenically an enviable destination for the walker, is less attractive for those who cannot arrange to be collected at the car park close to Invermark, for there are no buses and there is little if any accommodation available. Two alternative strategies are available: to return to Deeside (see below) or to continue to Strathmore. But it is imperative to realise that in both cases the result is an extremely long walk, suitable for only the fit and determined.

The Priest's Road – or Whisky Road – derives its names, as previously noted, from an energetic eighteenth-century minister and equally resourceful though more commercially motivated whisky-smugglers. It leaves the Glen Esk road near Invermark car park and proceeds to Dalbrack via Westbank and the western slopes of the Hill of Rowan, below the Earl of Dalhousie's curious monument, dedicated to seven dead members of his family and to himself and two others, 'when it shall please God to call them hence'.

The view northwards across Deeside to Glen Gairn from the slopes of Craig Vallich

The route climbs Garlet Hill, descends to and crosses the Berryhill Burn and threads its way by the steep trench of the Clash of Wirren to Stonyford in Glen Lethnot. Now the glen road has to be used, though there are signs of the original path across the West Water above Bridgend, and this route can be joined below Craig of Finnoch. From Bridgend there is no alternative to the road into Brechin, passing between the prehistoric hill-forts on the White and Brown Caterthuns.

The Firmounth Road: A Return to Deeside (16 miles/26km)

Take the Priest's Road to Westbank, then continue straight ahead to Tarfside, where there is an excellent folk museum. The Fungle, Firmounth and Birse Mounth Roads all start here, following the east bank of the Water of Tarf past Shinfur to the southern slopes of Tampie. Here the Firmounth Road keeps left and climbs to the summit of Tampie (2,363ft/720m) before passing St Colm's Well west of the summit of Gannoch and dropping down through forestry plantations to the Burn of Skinna and Glen Tanar. Alternative routes now make for Dinnet and Aboyne, both on the Deeside bus route.

Notes

Map   OS 1:50,000 sheet 44.
Further reading   C. Graham, *Portrait of Aberdeen and Deeside* (Robert Hale, 1972); Sir Edward Peck, *North-east Scotland* (Bartholomew 1981); Roger Smith (ed.), *Walking in Scotland* (Spurbooks, 1981).
Accommodation   A wide choice in Ballater; very scarce in Glen Esk.
Public transport   Ballater has seven buses a day along Deeside to Aberdeen; there are no services in upper Glen Esk. Brechin has an hourly service to Montrose, from where there are rail services to Aberdeen, Edinburgh and Glasgow.

(*opposite*) Invermark Castle and the River North Esk

34

THE CORRIEYAIRACK ROAD

Laggan Bridge to Fort Augustus 23 miles/37km

A magnificent walk, long but not excessively demanding, through the remote southern flanks of the Monadhliath ('grey mountains'). The route, with its wealth of historical associations, connects Speyside and the Great Glen, and rises to 2,507ft (764m) at the summit of the Corrieyairack Pass.

Historical Background

The 'road' over the Corrieyairack Pass is commonly referred to as General Wade's Military Road, but this is a gross over-simplification, for the route was in use centuries before Wade arrived on the scene, and his contribution forms only one part of the Corrieyairack's colourful history.

There is evidence that black cattle were already being driven over the Corrieyairack Pass on their way from Skye and northern Scotland to the tryst at Crieff (and later Falkirk) towards the end of the fifteenth century. It must have been quite a journey for the cattle: not just because they had to struggle up from Fort Augustus to the summit of the Corrieyairack, but also because they had already swum across the notoriously dangerous Kyle Rhea from Skye to the mainland.

The Monadhliath had already seen one pitched battle – William the Lion fought at Garvamore in 1187 – but a more notorious military use of the pass took place in February 1645, during the Covenanting wars. Montrose, trapped between a force of 5,000 men at Inverness and 3,000 Campbells at Inveraray, took his 1,500 men from Fort Augustus (then known as Kilcumin) over the Corrieyairack in deep snow before doubling back along Glen Roy and down to Inverlochy, where the unprepared Campbells were comprehensively slaughtered.

After the Highland uprisings of 1715 a road-building programme was begun under General Wade with the objective of bringing the Highlands under the control of the military. By 1730 there were roads connecting the string of forts in the Great Glen, from Fort William through Fort Augustus to Fort George near Inverness, and from Stirling north to Dalwhinnie and Fort George. Wade decided that the 1731 programme should consist of constructing a cross-country link between Dalwhinnie and Fort Augustus, using

216

The Spey Dam Reservoir and the hills above Garvamore

the drove route over the Corrieyairack Pass. Despite problems with the mountainous terrain, and six weeks of continuous rain, the military road was completed at the end of October 1731, at a cost of £3,281 4s 9d.

Ironically the first to benefit from the new road was Bonnie Prince Charlie, during the Jacobite rebellion of 1745. Having landed at Arisaig, Prince Charles Edward marched to Invergarry and the Corrieyairack. Sir John Cope, who had hurried north with the royal army to Dalwhinnie, chose not to engage the Jacobites and instead – disastrously – turned aside to Inverness to await reinforcements. Prince Charles Edward seized his opportunity to strike south towards Edinburgh and ultimately Derby. Cope later had to face an Inquiry (presided over by Wade) which came to the unanimous conclusion that he was 'unblameable'.

In April 1746 the remnants of the defeated Jacobite army hurried back northwards over the Corrieyairack, fearing retribution after Culloden – and rightly so, since the 'Bloody Butcher', the Duke of Cumberland, revelled in indiscriminate acts of revenge, confiscating stock, laying waste the country- side and slaughtering the innocent.

The Corrieyairack road was maintained by the military for almost a hundred years, before being handed over to the Commissioners for Highland Roads and Bridges in 1814. Following the construction of the Spean Bridge to Newtonmore road, however, the Commissioners elected to allow the upland section from Laggan Bridge westwards to fall into disuse. The bridges were still maintained, however, 'on account of their occasional accommodation as a passage for cattle'.

Hence the Corrieyairack became, once more, solely a drove road, and with the coming of the railways and the consequent decline of the droving trade it fell into almost total disuse. The last drove of cattle reached the summit of the pass in 1896, and the last sheep drove took place three years later. Now the Corrieyairack road lies abandoned, offering a classic walking route with, at worst, estate Land Rovers for company.

Description of the Route

Leave Laggan Bridge (NN614942) not by the surfaced road leading along the north bank of the Spey, but by the A86 southwards across the bridge. After a mile turn right on a lane leading to Dalchully House and cross Mashie Bridge, with Wade's military road now underfoot. Continue straight ahead on a rough track alongside the Spey when the Dalchully drive turns left, and follow the track as it rises gently away from the river to join the road from Laggan Bridge at a sharp bend above the Spey Dam.

The minor road now indicates Wade's route to Garvamore, though there are some variations; part of the old road lies underwater, and west of Shirrabeg there is an abandoned eighteenth-century bridge left high and dry by the diversion of its stream. Beyond Shirramore the road is flanked by pines to the left and there are fine views into Glen Shirra, with an excellent outlook towards Carn Liath across Loch Crunachdan. Then the road curves around a hillock to reveal Garvamore, an extraordinarily isolated farm complex in the Spey flood plain almost at the end of the metalled road.

Garbhamór, as it was then known, was the point at which Wade's road crossed the Spey, and St George's Bridge, completed in 1732, still stands. Two-arched and 150ft long, it is one of Wade's finest memorials. The former kingshouse (ie on the king's highway), originally a barracks and later an inn, at Garbhamór still stands, although the fabric of the building has been allowed to deteriorate.

The walk to Garvamore has involved virtually no climbing, but beyond St George's Bridge the ascent of the Corrieyairack begins. The road climbs above forestry and then rejoins the fast-flowing Spey as it heads for Mealgarbha (Melgarve), with long, straight alignments emphasising its military origins. At Melgarve the track to Glen Roy leaves on the left; the Corrieyairack road, now a rough hill-track policed rather disconcertingly by a line of pylons, keeps straight on, climbing steadily on towards the vast

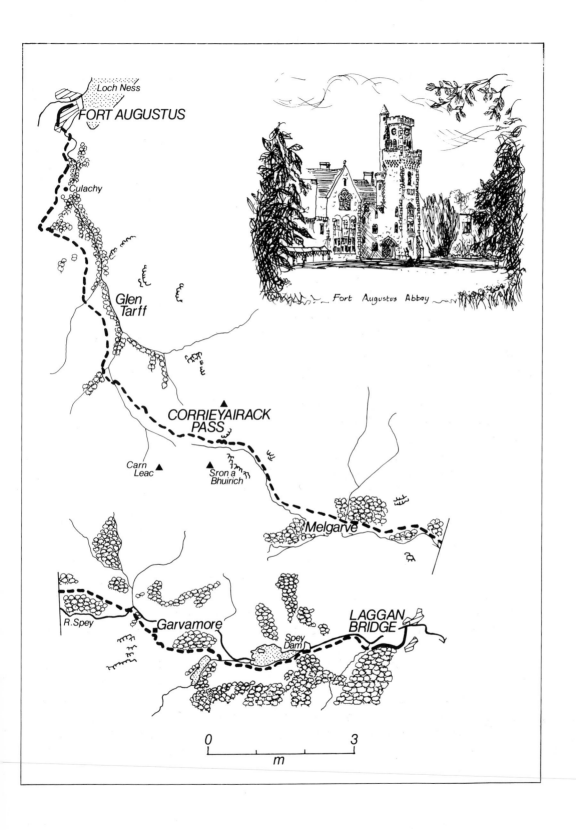

Loch Ness

FORT AUGUSTUS

Culachy

Glen
Tarff

Fort Augustus Abbey

CORRIEYAIRACK
PASS

Carn
Leac

Sron a
Bhuirich

Melgarve

R. Spey

Garvamore

Spey
Dam

LAGGAN
BRIDGE

0   3

m

hollow of Corrie Yairack, with Corrieyairack Hill towering above the corrie.

The hardest part of the walk begins in the corrie, as the track climbs steeply for some 500ft to the summit of the pass. But the ascent is eased very considerably by Wade's skilful use of well-constructed zigzags, efficiently drained and sturdily buttressed by stone and mortar. Originally there were eighteen zigzags, though now only thirteen remain, and they are falling slowly into disrepair, although the ascent is still perfectly feasible.

The summit of the Corrieyairack Pass, which divides Corrieyairack Hill and Carn Leac at 2,507ft (764m), is on a fine day an exhilarating place to be; but it can also be dangerously exposed to the elements, and due allowance for this should be made in planning the walk. The view – regrettably interrupted by the inevitable pylons – is wide-ranging and of high quality. To the right is the Moray Firth, to the left lie Knoydart and the Cuillin of Skye, and between them are the Kintail and Affric peaks, topped by Carn Eige.

Not everyone has been impressed by the summit scene, however. Pennant, writing in 1769, was more concerned to warn of dreadful snowstorms, remarking that 'people often perish on the summit'. Sixty years later Anderson described the 'dreariness of this forlorn region', the cutting blasts of wind and the winter snow. In fact the Monadhliath, unable to offer any challenges to the rock-climber and generally ignored by walkers as well,

Loch Ness and the military road above Culachy House

The bouldery western end of the Corrieyairack Road

contains not only the Corrieyairack road but also ridge walks of high quality with superb distant views.

The descent from the wild, untamed environs of the Corrieyairack Pass into the delightfully wooded Glen Tarff is well graded and easy. The road crosses Allt Coire Uchdachan on the surviving military bridge, then crosses its sister Allt Lagan a Bhainne on a Bailey bridge of much more recent vintage, contours round below Carn Bad na Circe and, still in close company with the pylons, loses height steadily whilst staying well above the River Tarff.

The first of two steeper sections occurs as the road zigzags down a hillside to cross the Culachy burn some way above the well-hidden Culachy Falls, but after climbing the opposite slope the Corrieyairack road returns to its gentle progress towards the Great Glen. Shortly after the Knollbuck track comes in from the left the proximity of the Great Glen becomes apparent, with a glorious view along the length of Loch Ness. Fort Augustus, too, is now close at hand, the abbey towers prominent in the woods at the head of the loch.

The track swings left and, after passing through a tall gate sometimes adorned with warnings of deer culling in progress, meets the second of the steeper sections and drops more abruptly past the secretive Culachy House.

In places the slaty bedrock has been exposed, and elsewhere the track (clearly much used at this western end) consists of rough bouldery scree.

Loch Ness still dominates the view ahead at this point, but there is little time for relaxation on the rough and treacherous boulder slope leading down to the Ardachy road, where a prominent sign advertises 'Wade's Road to Laggan'. From here it is only 1½ miles to Fort Augustus and the end of Wade's road, with a variety of routes possible for this last section, one of them passing the ancient Kilcumin burial ground, last resting place of Robert Burns' carpenter friend John Anderson.

Fort Augustus (NH378093) was formerly called Kilcumin – literally 'the church of St Chumein' – after the seventh Abbot of Iona, a follower of St Columba, but with Hanoverian arrogance was renamed Fort Augustus in honour of the Duke of Cumberland, the victor at the battle of Culloden. The ancient fort behind the Lovat Arms Hotel was superseded in the 1730s by General Wade's fort on the promontory at the head of Loch Ness. The fort, captured after a three-day siege by the Jacobites in 1745, was later restored, but the garrison left a century or so later and in 1876 the Order of St Benedict took over, and constructed Fort Augustus Abbey, part of which now houses a Roman Catholic school.

There is a museum in the abbey grounds, but the two main attractions of Fort Augustus are the Caledonian Canal, built by Thomas Telford between 1803 and 1847 and now used by pleasure boats and a few fishing vessels, which can be seen climbing the flight of locks in the village, and the legendary Loch Ness monster, a useful tourist asset but one which, perhaps surprisingly, is not over-exploited.

Notes

Maps   OS 1:50,000 sheets 34 and 35.

Further reading   Ian Finlay, *The Central Highlands* (Batsford, 1976); W. Douglas Simpson, *Portrait of the Highlands* (Robert Hale, 1969); William Taylor, *The Military Roads in Scotland* (David & Charles, 1976).

Public transport   This is very scarce in upper Speyside, but with some ingenuity it is possible to complete the walk in a day using Inverness as a base. Take the morning train south to Newtonmore, where on certain days there is a connection with the Highland Omnibuses service to Laggan Bridge (the service seems to be permanently 'subject to review', so it would be prudent to check that it still operates). It is possible to wait at Laggan Bridge and connect with the post-bus from Dalwhinnie, which goes on to Garvamore and (three times a week) to Melgarve. Fort Augustus has fairly frequent services on the Fort William to Inverness route.

Accommodation   Hotels and some bed and breakfast are available at both Laggan Bridge and Fort Augustus.

35

BRIDGE OF ORCHY TO FORT WILLIAM BY MILITARY ROAD

Bridge of Orchy to Fort William 28 miles/45km

For almost its entire length this testing walk follows the military road between Stirling and Fort William, constructed between 1750 and 1752 by Major Caulfeild, who had succeeded General Wade ten years previously. The Devil's Staircase, between Altnafeadh and Kinlochleven, reaches 1,800ft and some parts of the route can be exposed in rough weather, but the surface is good and the route-finding easy – the more so since much of the route became part of the controversial West Highland Way, Scotland's first long-distance footpath.

Historical Background

Although the walk follows an eighteenth-century military road parts of the route have a far longer history, having formed one section of the drove route from Skye to the trysts at Crieff and Falkirk. The military route took over long stretches of the drove road, yet was itself superseded during the nineteenth century by a new road at a generally lower altitude – a reflection not only of the harsh winter climate but of inadequacies in the army's construction techniques.

Military roads in the Highlands were a response to the risings in 1715 and 1745, and especially to General Wade's report that the area could not be brought under control without adequate communications. Wade himself supervised the first roads to be built, but later Major Toby Caulfeild took over and it was he who set about providing a route between Stirling and Fort William.

Work began in 1748, but it was two years later before the central section, including the notoriously steep Devil's Staircase above Altnafeadh, was started. In May 1752 the final section, from Inveroran to Kingshouse across the Black Mount and the edge of Rannoch Moor, was commenced, with about 1,100 troops employed on the work. Appalling weather meant that the road was left unfinished, and it was June 1753 before it was actually complete.

The ascent of the Devil's Staircase was exposed and arduous, and as early as 1785 this part of the road was abandoned and replaced by a road through Glencoe to Ballachulish Ferry and along the shores of Loch Linnhe. The military road was repaired, under Telford's direction, in the early years of the nineteenth century, and a new line was chosen across the Black Mount. The road was still used by drovers (in 1803 William and Dorothy Wordsworth saw a southbound drove at Inveroran), and rights of pasturage existed here until 1846. In the second half of the nineteenth century, as the droving trade declined, sheep (rather than cattle) were still being driven from Kingshouse across the Black Mount to Bridge of Orchy and the south.

Description of the Route

Start this walk early on a June morning if you intend to complete it in a day (the first train from Glasgow will deposit you at Bridge of Orchy station at about 8 o'clock). Apart from the station and the imposing hotel there is virtually nothing at Bridge of Orchy (NN297396), except for the eighteenth-century bridge over the River Orchy and a recent addition, a West Highland Way noticeboard. This promises company on the walk, and efficient waymarking, and on this popular route both promises are likely to be kept.

There is an immediate choice, between the single-track A8005, which has the advantages of easy walking and certainty of arrival at Forest Lodge, or climbing the ladder stile on the left to follow the true line of the military road, which climbs higher across the prominent spur of Mam Carraigh. This is much the pleasanter route, though it has recently been hemmed in by forestry plantations, to the detriment of the splendid panorama of Rannoch Moor across Loch Tulla. The stone foundations of the military road can be seen in places, so much so that the military road between Bridge of Orchy and Inveroran is scheduled as an ancient monument.

After ½ mile there is a fine zigzag as the military road gains height; from this point there is a memorable view of Beinn Dòrain across the Orchy valley. A mile or so later the military road rejoins the A8005 – the old Glencoe road – just to the east of Inveroran Hotel, once a staging-post for the coach service between Fort William and Glasgow and before that a stance for the drovers on their way to Falkirk Tryst. Duncan Ban MacIntyre, one of the finest Gaelic poets, was born near Inveroran and is perhaps best known for his poems celebrating the 'glorious ground' of Beinn Dòrain.

Beyond the tree belts around Inveroran Hotel – a real haven in the heavy rain which can linger here – follow the present road across Victoria Bridge to its conclusion at Forest Lodge. Cars can go no further, but walkers have a choice between the old Glencoe road, an unsurfaced track which was the main road until the present A82 was surfaced in 1932, and the military road, which follows a marginally higher course for much of the way.

Both routes traverse the slopes beneath the hills of the Black Mount, topped by Meall a' Bhùirdh (3,636ft/1,108m) and Clach Leathad (3,602ft/ 1,098m), while away to the east stretches Rannoch Moor, strikingly desolate yet studded with sparkling lochans, and the much bigger expanses of Loch Bà and Loch Laidon. Rannoch Moor, an expanse of peat overlying granite, was once heavily wooded – part of the ancient Caledonian Forest – and remnants of the old pine forest survive in the Black Wood of Rannoch, near Bà Cottage.

Keep to the old military road as it passes Lochan Mhic Pheadair Ruaidh and makes for Bà Bridge, a good viewpoint for Coireach a' Bà, acknowledged

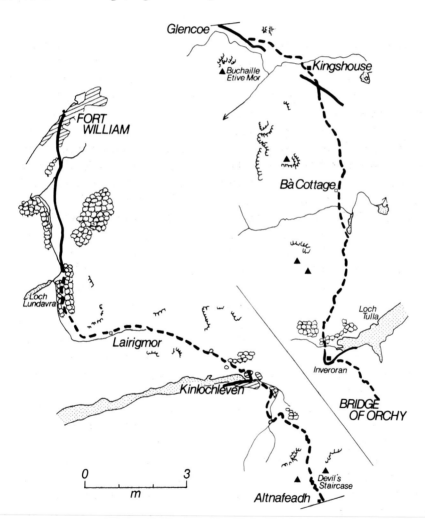

Inveroran Hotel

as the largest corrie in Scotland. After a further ¼ mile the ruined Bà Cottage
and the lush green marking its cattle stance can be seen on the left, then the
military road and the old Glencoe road (which is here pleasanter to walk
along) diverge again for a while, reuniting just before the climbing hut
known as Blackrock Cottage. This is a major skiing area, and the White
Corries ski-lifts can be picked out high on the left.

A lane now points the way to and across the A82, heading for the
Kingshouse Hotel. East of the main road the lane is particularly badly
surfaced and it makes for an unusual approach to 'Scotland's oldest inn', a
comfortable hotel which has perhaps been too heavily modernised to retain
its air of history. Yet it originated as a camp for the troops building the
military road, developed into an inn known as a kingshouse because it was
on the king's highway, and later served as a stance for the drovers.

Rain clouds approach Buachaille Etive Mór, seen here from the military road near the Kingshouse Hotel

Depart from Kingshouse across a bridge at the back of the hotel, follow the surfaced lane past the inconspicuous ruins of Queenshouse and then look for the West Highland Way sign as a guide to the route across the lower slopes of Beinn a' Chrùlaiste above and to the right of the main road as far as Altnafeadh (yet another cattle stance) and the bottom of the Devil's Staircase.

The route is signposted to Kinlochleven, but is obvious anyway and is badly worn in places. Nevertheless it is a wonderful experience, tracing the military road through a series of zigzags to the summit of the pass, at about 1,800ft between Stob Mhic Mhartuin and Beinn Bheag. The reward on the way up is the retrospective sight of Buachaille Etive Mór and Glencoe, and at the top is the astonishing sight of Ben Nevis and the Mamores to the north.

On the way down to Kinlochleven a prominent feature is the Blackwater Reservoir, constructed between 1904 and 1907 to provide power for the

Loch Lundavra

Kinlochleven aluminium works. Somewhat older are the traces of the military road, especially the paved cross-drains which took away much of the water from the marshy area around the crossing of the Allt a' Choire Odhair-Mhóir. Two more miles and the route passes the aluminium works and enters Kinlochleven, neatly summed up by Hamish MacInnes as 'a deplorable town in a delectable setting'. A mere hamlet before the arrival of the aluminium industry, Kinlochleven was planned in a hurry and it shows.

Take the stony track from Kinlochleven to Mamore Lodge, used by King Edward VII as a shooting lodge, and turn left along the old military road, with fine views along Loch Leven. The road passes the ruins of Tigh-na-Sleubhaich and then Lairigmór, a wonderfully remote situation for what was a stalker's cottage. The way here lies along a green track and it can be wet after rain. The military road then follows the valley of the Allt na Lairige Móire west and then north towards Blàr a' Chaoruinn and the metalled road, ending with a rough, forested section which can be trying.

On the way down to Blàr a' Chaoruinn there is an enjoyable prospect over to the left of the wild and lonely Loch Lundavra (an Anglicised form of Lochan Lunn Dà-Bhrà). Lulach, Macbeth's cousin and successor, reputedly lived on an island in the loch; even less likely is the legend of a resident water bull. Yet Lundavra on a misty day is that sort of place.

The remainder of the route is straightforward, along Lundavra Road and through the crofts making up the hamlet of Blarmachfoldach to Fort William. At the top of the hill leading down to the town is a picnic site with marvellous views across Loch Linnhe to the low hills beyond. Finally, descend through Upper Achintore into Fort William itself, joining the coast road just south of the unremarkable town centre (NN098738). Nowadays the town depends on its aluminium factory, pulp mill and distillery, together with tourism; previously it was a garrison town (once known as Maryburgh) which grew up around the fort which replaced Inverlochy Castle. Only the entrance gate of the fort survives, re-erected at a cemetery north of the town centre, but the name has survived as an appropriate reminder of its military origins.

Notes

Maps OS 1:63,360 Tourist Map (Ben Nevis and Glen Coe), or 1:50,000 sheets 41 and 50.

Further reading Tom Hunter, *A Guide to the West Highland Way* (Constable, 1979); Hamish MacInnes, *West Highland Walks: One* (Hodder & Stoughton, 1979); William Taylor, *The Military Roads in Scotland* (David & Charles, 1976).

Accommodation The Kingshouse Hotel is beautifully situated as a half-way house; alternatively there is quite a lot of cheap, friendly bed and breakfast accommodation in Kinlochleven. Fort William is liberally supplied with all types of accommodation.

Public transport Trains and buses from Glasgow to Fort William stop at Bridge of Orchy (three trains per day, two buses). The bus also passes Kingshouse road end. Kinlochleven has a fairly regular bus connection to Fort William.

INDEX